The Essentials of Project Management

The Essentials of Project Management

Fourth Edition

DENNIS LOCK

GOWER

Published by
Gower Publishing Limited
Wey Court East
Union Road
Farnham
Surrey GU9 7PT
England

Gower Publishing Company
110 Cherry Street
Suite 3-1
Burlington, VT 05401-3818
USA

Dennis Lock has asserted his moral right under the Copyright, Designs and Patents Act, 1988, to be identified as the author of this work.

British Library Cataloguing in Publication Data
A catalogue record for this book is available from the British Library

   ISBN: 9781472442536 (pbk)
   ISBN: 9781472442543 (ePDF)
   ISBN: 9781472442550 (ePUB)

The Library of Congress has cataloged the printed edition as follows:
Lock, Dennis.
  The essentials of project management / by Dennis Lock. -- Fourth Edition.
    pages cm
  Includes bibliographical references and index.
  ISBN 978-1-4724-4253-6 (pbk) -- ISBN 978-1-4724-4254-3 (ebook) -- ISBN 978-1-4724-4255-0 (epub) 1. Project management. I. Title.
  T56.8.L57 2014
  658.4'04--dc23

                                              2014011279

1007302260

Printed in the United Kingdom by Henry Ling Limited, at the Dorset Press, Dorchester, DT1 1HD

Contents

List of Figures   *ix*
Preface   *xiii*

1   Introduction to Projects and their Management   1
Project Fundamentals   1
Project Characteristics   1
People and Organizations   3
Project Life Cycles and Life Histories   4
Factors Relevant to Success or Failure   5
Relationship Between the Three Primary Objectives   6
Perceptions of Project Success or Failure Beyond the Three
    Primary Objectives   9
Benefits Realization   11
Principal Organizations Representing the Project
    Management Profession   12
References   13

2   Defining the Project Task   15
Projects Which are Impossible to Define Accurately   16
Checklists   17
Defining the Project Scope   20
The Contractor's Strategy   21
Specifications for Internally Funded Development Projects   23
The Project Specification and Version Control   26

3   Estimating the Project Costs   29
Cost Elements   29
Accuracy of Cost Estimates   30
Standard Estimating Tables   31
Compiling the Task List   32
Documenting the Cost Estimates   32
Collecting Departmental Estimates   34
The Estimating Abilities of Different People   35
Estimates for Material and Equipment Costs   36
Below the Line Costs   38
Reviewing the Cost Estimates   40

4   Managing Risk   **43**
Identifying the Possible Risks   43
Risk Appraisal and Analysis   44
Risk Register   46
Methods for Dealing with Risks   47
Obtaining Insurance   50

5   Organizing the Project   **51**
Matrix Organizations   51
Project Team Organization   55
Team or Matrix: which Organization is Best?   57
Hybrid Organizations   59
Contract Matrix Organizations   60
Joint Venture Projects   61
The Project Manager   62
Project Management Office (PMO)   65

6   Work Breakdown Structures   **67**
The WBS Concept   67
Coding Systems   72
Benefits of a Logical Coding System   75
Choosing a Coding System   79
What Happens when the Customer Says 'You Shall Use
    my Coding System!'?   80

7   Planning the Timescale   **83**
Bar Charts   83
Critical Path Analysis   87
Two Different Network Notation Systems   87
Critical Path Networks Using Arrow Diagrams   88
Precedence Network Diagrams   91
Planning the Furniture Project by Critical Path Network   94
Level of Detail in Network Diagrams   95
Milestones   99
Is the Predicted Timescale too Long?   99
Early Consideration of Resource Constraints   100

8   Scheduling Project Resources   **103**
Resource Scheduling   103
The Role of Network Analysis in Resource Scheduling   104
Introducing the Garage Project   104
Garage Project Network Planning   107
A First Look at the Garage Project Resource Schedule   108
Float   109

	Garage Project Resource Scheduling	112
	Computer Scheduling of the Garage and Other Projects	115
	Recapitulation	121

9	**Implementing the Project Plan**	**123**
	Project Authorization	123
	Preliminary Organization of the Project	124
	Physical Preparations and Organization	128
	Getting Work Started	130
	Detailed Plans and Work Instructions	131
	Managing Progress	133
	Progress Monitoring and Schedule Updating	134
	When the News is Bad	137
	Progress Meetings	139
	Project Progress Reports	141

10	**Managing Purchasing**	**143**
	Outline of the Purchasing Function	143
	Specifying the Goods to be Purchased	144
	Early Ordering of Long-lead Items	146
	Choosing the Best Supplier	146
	Purchase Order	150
	Expediting	152
	Shipping, Port and Customs Formalities	154
	Goods Receipt	155
	Shortages	155
	Vendors' Documents	156

11	**Managing Changes**	**159**
	The Impact of Changes in Relation to the Project Life Cycle	159
	Classification of Changes	160
	Change Authorization Procedures	160
	Registration and Progressing	162
	Formal Procedures for External Change Requests	163
	Formal Procedure for Internal Change Requests	165
	Design Freeze	167
	The Interchangeability Rule	167
	Emergency Modifications	167

12	**Managing Costs**	**173**
	A Checklist of Cost Management Factors	173
	Cost Budgets	174
	Milestone Analysis	176

A Simple Performance Analysis Method for
    Design Engineering   180
An Outline of Earned Value Analysis   180
Effect of Changes on Earned Value Analysis   185
The Project Ledger Concept   186
Predicting Profitability for a Project   187
Managing Cash Flow   189
Closing the Project Down   192

13   **Corporate Managers' Support for the Project
        Manager**   **195**
Costs and Benefits of Project Management   195
Active Support from Senior Management for
    Project Management   198
Reference   201

Select Bibliography   *203*
Index   *207*

List of Figures

1.1 The active part of a project life cycle   4
1.2 Typical life cycle (life history) of a large project   5

2.1 Definition of a large project from initial concept to completion   15
2.2 Part of a definition checklist for a mining project   19
2.3 Initial task checklist for a management change project   20

3.1 Elements of a cost estimate for a typical industrial project   30
3.2 A general purpose estimating form, particularly applicable to
     manufacturing projects   33
3.3 Cost estimating form for purchased materials and bought
     equipment on a capital project   38

4.1 Part of a failure, mode and effect analysis (FMEA)   45
4.2 Failure, mode, effect and criticality analysis (FMECA)   46
4.3 Example of a risk register (or risk log) format   47
4.4 Insurance options and obligations   49

5.1 A coordination matrix for a manufacturing project   52
5.2 A matrix organization for multiple manufacturing projects   53
5.3 A matrix organization for mining and petrochemical projects   54
5.4 A project team organization   55
5.5 Project team versus a balance matrix   59
5.6 A hybrid organization   60
5.7 A contract matrix organization   61
5.8 One form of joint venture organization for a large project   62

6.1 Simplified WBS for an automobile project   67
6.2 WBS for a national charity fundraising week   68
6.3 Part of the upper WBS levels for a copper mine   70
6.4 Alternative WBS patterns for a large wedding project   71
6.5 Part of the WBS and coding structure for a
     radiocommunications project   74
6.6 Detail from the radiocommunications project WBS   74
6.8 Codes used by a mining engineering company   76
6.7 Codes used by a heavy engineering company   76

6.9   Coded data in a database brings order from chaos   77

7.1   Task list for the furniture project   84
7.2   Bar chart (or Gantt chart) for the furniture project   85
7.3   Linked bar chart for the furniture project   86
7.4   The elements of an arrow critical path network diagram   89
7.5   An activity in precedence notation   92
7.6   The elements of a precedence critical path network diagram   92
7.7   Furniture project: activity-on-arrow network diagram   95
7.8   Furniture project: precedence network diagram   96
7.9   Time analysis for the furniture project   96
7.10 Activity constraint options in precedence networks   100

8.1   Garage project task list   105
8.2   Garage project network diagram   106
8.3   Garage project critical path network time analysis   108
8.4   Garage project bar chart and histogram (resource aggregation) 109
8.5   Garage project: float analysis of activity G016   110
8.6   Three different resource usage patterns for the garage project 113
8.7   Time-limited versus resource-limited priority rules   115
8.8   Garage project resource-limited schedule (data from Primavera) 116
8.9   Garage project cost and time graphs, with resource-limited
      scheduling   117
8.10 Garage project resource usage forecast   118
8.11 Seven logical steps to a practical project resource schedule   121

9.1   A project authorization form used by a mining engineering
      company   125
9.2   Two useful matrix charts   126
9.3   Fragment of a checklist for an overseas construction site   129
9.4   A cybernetic control loop, an example of management by
      exception   134

10.1 Purchasing cycle for a high-value project item   144
10.2 Some purchasing procedures applicable to projects   145
10.3 A typical sealed bids process   148
10.4 A bid summary example   149
10.5 An inspection and expediting report example   153
10.6 Example of a materials shortage list   156

11.1 The cost of a change in relation to the project life cycle   159
11.2 Project variation order   163
11.3 An engineering change request   166

12.1   Data for a milestone chart   178
12.2   Project cost and achievement comparison using milestones   178
12.3   A project cost report that shows predictions based on earned
       value analysis   188
12.4   Logical steps required to calculate a net cash flow schedule   190
12.5   Net cash flow schedule for a construction project   191
12.6   Project closure notice with checklist   193

Preface

The first edition of this book resulted from a suggestion from Gower that I might produce a précis of my larger work, *Project Management*. This recognized that not all students and practising project managers needed the comprehensive coverage of the larger work.

I have always been aware of the need to keep this book of essentials in step with its mother text and other project management development. So this fourth edition is the junior complement to the tenth edition of *Project Management*, which was published in 2013. It is intended for practising managers, and for students where project management is one module in their degree syllabus.

Chapter 13 is new for this edition. Project management cannot succeed without support from senior managers. It is they who authorize the people and resources to carry out the function. It is easy (and not uncommon) to regard this expenditure as an unnecessary addition to overheads. But project management, when efficient and not overstaffed, delivers value for money. In more than one company I have seen big performance improvements with projects completed early and well under budget as a direct result of project management training, effective organization, dedication of the project staff and logical planning. None of those savings and benefits would have been possible without active and enthusiastic support from senior executives.

I am always grateful to serious reviewers and I am particularly indebted this time to Max Wideman for reviewing two of my other recent books thoroughly and sympathetically. His comments on those works led me to make some corrections in this revised text.

Dennis Lock
St Albans
2014

1 *Introduction to Projects and their Management*

Human-led projects are hardly new, as wonders of the ancient world testify. But their progress was usually managed by the engineers and architects who designed them. It is only in relatively recent years that project management has become recognized as a specialized branch of management, with its own professional associations, qualifications and a comprehensive and expanding methodology. Anyone interested in the development of project management should consult Morris (1997).

PROJECT FUNDAMENTALS

The purpose of project management is to plan, organize and control all activities so that the project is completed as successfully as possible in spite of all the difficulties and risks. The buzzwords here are *deliverables* (the expected project benefits) and *stakeholders* (organizations and people with any significant interest in the project and its deliverables). Francis Hartman believed that a successful project is one that makes all its stakeholders happy (Hartman, 2000). Well, maybe that's not always possible but he makes a good point.

Every significant project should begin with a definition and business case that defines the project and forecasts the investment required and the expected benefits. That business case (sometimes called a business plan) should be approved before any money and other resources are committed to the project. For a large project preparation of the business case itself can need considerable money and other resources.

Project definition is considered in greater detail in Chapter 2. Every business case requires an estimate of project costs and an assessment of the possible risks, and those topics are discussed in Chapters 3 and 4, respectively.

PROJECT CHARACTERISTICS

The principal characteristic of any project is its novelty. It is a step into the unknown, fraught with risk and uncertainty. No two projects are ever exactly alike.

Even a repeated project will differ in one or more commercial, administrative, or physical aspects from its predecessor.

Four Main Project Types

Projects can loosely be classified under four main headings (these definitions are my own).

Civil engineering, construction, petrochemical, mining and quarrying projects

These generally involve work on a site which is exposed to the elements and remote from the contractor's head office. Such projects incur special risks and problems of organization and communication. They often require massive capital investment, and they deserve (but do not always get) rigorous management of progress, finance and quality. The amount of finance and other resources may be too great for one contractor, in which case the organization and communications are further complicated by the participation of several contractors, working together in some kind of joint venture.

Manufacturing projects

These are projects for new product research and development or to produce a piece of equipment or machinery, ship, aircraft, land vehicle, or some other item of specially designed hardware. Manufacturing projects are often conducted in factories or other home-based environments, where it should be possible to exercise on-the-spot management and provide an optimum working environment.

Management and business change projects

These projects prove the point that every company, whatever its size, can expect to need project management expertise at least once in its lifetime. These are the projects that happen when companies relocate, develop and introduce new IT or communications systems, prepare for a trade exhibition, set up a training programme, restructure the organization, plan a spectacular celebration and so on. There is no tangible product.

Scientific research projects

Here I mean projects for pure scientific research (not the more predictable research and development projects intended to result in a new product).Pure research projects can consume vast sums of money, last for many years, and either result in a dramatically profitable discovery or prove to have been a complete waste of time and money. Sometimes the intended outcomes are not realized but an unexpected benefit results. Thus pure research projects carry extremely high risk. They aim to extend the boundaries of current human knowledge and their end objectives are usually difficult or impossible to define.However, some form of control (project management) must be applied to prevent the waste of potentially vast sums of money. Clearly budgets have to be set in line with available funding. A process called *stage-gating* is one answer to this problem. This requires that the project sponsors review progress at regular intervals or stages (say, every six months). If a review shows that the research continues to show promise, funds can be released for the next six months of research. However, if funds run short, or if the research appears to be going nowhere useful, funds can be withdrawn and the project stopped – a process commonly known as 'pulling the plug'.

This book is generally concerned with projects that can be defined, as explained in the first three categories listed above.

PEOPLE AND ORGANIZATIONS

Customer and Contractor

Many projects are carried out by a contractor for an external organization (the customer). The customer and contractor agree terms and prices in a contract. However, this arrangement is clouded for some management change projects, where much of the work is conducted by employees of the organization itself. Then the organization is both contractor and its own customer. For simplicity, I shall use the term *contractor* throughout this book to describe whoever carries out the project work and *customer* to describe the owner of the project, regardless of whether the customer and contractor reside in the same organization.

The Project Manager

A project manager is usually imagined as a person, but it can be a company or other organization that acts as a managing contractor on behalf of a project customer. Whatever the case, there will usually be one individual who can be identified as carrying responsibility for the success of the project. And, usually, that person will be called the project manager.

Today's project manager has ready access to an increasing range of cost-effective tools for planning and controlling a project. The most successful manager will be capable of choosing and using those techniques which best suit the particular project. But there is clearly far more to managing a project than the application of techniques and procedures. Project management embodies a whole framework of logical planning and decisions, perceptiveness, the liberal application of common sense, appropriate organization, effective commercial and financial management, painstaking attention to documentation, and above all the ability to lead and motivate people.

PROJECT LIFE CYCLES AND LIFE HISTORIES

Most authorities and writers, when they talk about the life cycle of a project, refer to the period that begins with the authorization of project work and ends with the handover of the desired product to the customer. Although that view can be too simplistic, it is the part of projects that is of most concern to project managers (and which is covered in this book). Figure 1.1 shows that the activities which take place during this period form a true cycle, because they begin and end with the customer.

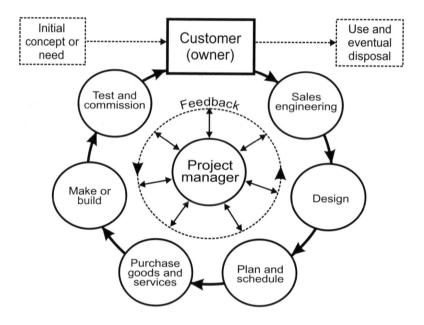

1.1 The active part of a project life cycle

Travelling clockwise round the cycle reveals a number of steps or phases. In practice, these phases usually overlap, so that the boundaries between them are blurred. For example, some project purchasing and other work can usually start before the design phase is complete.

The view of a project life cycle shown in Figure 1.1 is too simplistic for most projects because it ignores everything that happens before the start of actual work and takes no account of what happens to the project after its delivery to the customer. For a more complete picture we have to consider not only the project life cycle as seen by the project manager, but also the entire life history of the project from its initial conception to final death and disposal. Figure 1.2 shows this more complete view of a project life history.

Project phase	Five-year periods				
1 Original concept	◆				
2 Feasibility study	▬				
3 Business case	■				
4 Risk assessment	■				
5 Public enquiry	▬				
6 Authorization	◆				
7 Organization	▮				
8 Planning	■				
9 Design	▬				
10 Procurement	▬				
11 Fulfilment	▬				
12 Test/commission	■				
13 Handover	◆				
14 Economic life		▬▬▬▬▬			
15 Disposal					◆

Project management phases ◀————▶

1.2   Typical life cycle (life history) of a large project

Many writers limit their account of the project life cycle or life history to phases 6 to 13, because these are the phases that usually come under the control of the project manager. They constitute the most active period of the project life history (sometimes called the fulfilment period). This period corresponds in most respects to the life cycle in Figure 1.1. The chapters in this book are arranged as far as possible in this life cycle sequence.

FACTORS RELEVANT TO SUCCESS OR FAILURE

The success of the contractor and the project manager will usually be judged according to how well they achieve the three primary objectives, which are usually acknowledged as:

1. Project completion within the approved cost budget;
2. The project finished on time;
3. Good performance, which requires that the project satisfies its specification and delivers the intended benefits.

Factors for achieving these three objectives include the following:

- Good project definition and a sound business case at the outset;
- Appropriate choice of project strategy;

- Strong support for the project and its manager from higher management;
- Availability of sufficient funds and other resources;
- Firm control of changes to the authorized project;
- Technical competence;
- A sound quality culture throughout the organization;
- A suitable organization structure;
- Appropriate regard for the health and safety of everyone connected with the project;
- Good project communications;
- Well-motivated staff;
- Quick and fair resolution of conflict.

These issues are all important for good project management.Some projects fail to satisfy all their objectives yet can be considered, in retrospect, to have been successful. For example, the Eurotunnel was seriously overspent yet those of us who use it would consider it a great success.

RELATIONSHIP BETWEEN THE THREE PRIMARY OBJECTIVES

It is occasionally necessary to identify one of the three primary objectives as being of special importance. This emphasis can affect the priority given to the allocation of scarce resources and the way in which management attention is concentrated. It can also influence the choice of project organization structure (discussed in Chapter 5).

A management decision to place greater emphasis on achieving one or two of these objectives must sometimes be made at the expense of the remaining objectives. Such a trade-off decision can be illustrated by placing a spot or blob within a triangle which has one primary objective placed at each of its corners (shown in Figure 1.3). For example, if cost is the greatest consideration, the blob will be placed in the cost corner. If all the objectives are regarded as equal (balanced), the blob can be omitted or put in the middle of the triangle.

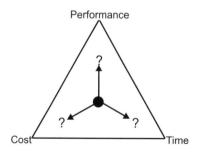

1.3 The triangle of objectives (after Dr Martin Barnes)

A project for a charitable organization with limited funds would have controlled costs as the project manager's chief concern. Industries such as aerospace and nuclear power generation have to place high emphasis on safety and reliability, so performance should be the most important objective. A project to set up and stock a stand at a trade exhibition, for which the date has been announced and the venue booked, is so dependent on meeting the time objective that it might be necessary to overspend on budgets to avoid missing the date.

The Quality/cost Relationship

It is a mistake to believe that there can be a simple and acceptable trade-off between *quality* and cost. Those who promote total quality management argue, correctly, that quality can be achieved without extra cost. However, there is an even more fundamental reason why quality cannot be downgraded or compromised to save money. This becomes clear when we accept the definition of quality as a service or product that is 'fit for the purpose for which it was intended'. No contractor or project manager should ever contemplate a result that is not 'fit for purpose'. Therefore downgrading quality is not an option. That is why 'performance' or 'level of specification' is placed at the corner of the triangle of objectives rather than 'quality'.

This distinction between 'quality' and 'specification' is illustrated by the following example. Suppose that the initial estimates for a new building are too high and that construction costs must be reduced. One option might be to build on relatively simple foundations instead of using deep sunk piles, which could save thousands of pounds. But if the ground conditions demand piling for the building to be safe, that cost-saving option is ruled out on the grounds of reliability and safety. It would compromise quality and is not a viable option. The building would not be fit for its intended purpose.

However, suppose that the same developer reviews the specification for interior finishes and finds that marble floors could be replaced with carpeted floors at a substantial cost saving. The floors would still be serviceable and fit for purpose. Carpeting would, therefore, be an option that would not compromise quality. *Quality* has not been changed, but the *specification* has.

The Time/cost Relationship

TIME IS MONEY!
(Benjamin Franklin, in Advice to a Young Tradesman, 1748)

There is usually a direct and very important relationship between time and money. If a project runs late its original cost estimates are almost certain to be overspent. A project costs money during every day of its existence, working or non-working, weekday or weekend, from day one of the programme right through until the last payment has exchanged hands. These costs arise for a variety of reasons, some of which will now be explained.

The Effect of Project Delays on Direct Costs

The *variable* or *direct* costs of labour and materials are time-related in several ways. Cost inflation is one factor, so that a job started and finished later than planned might cost more than the original estimate because of price rises in materials and increases in wages, salaries and other costs.

There are other less obvious causes where late working implies inefficient working, perhaps through lost time or waiting time (often the result of materials shortages, missing information, or poor planning, communications and organization). If any project task takes longer to perform than its planned duration, it is probable that the budgeted man-hours will be exceeded. This is true not only for a single task, but also for the project as a whole.

The Effect of Project Delays on Indirect (Overhead) Costs

The *fixed* or *overhead* costs of management, administration, accommodation, services and general facilities will be incurred day-by-day, every day, regardless of work done, until the project is finished. If the project runs late, these costs will have to be borne for a longer period than planned. They will then exceed their budget.

The Effect of Project Delays on the Costs of Financing

Another important time-related cost is financing. Where the contractor has an overdraft at the bank or relies on other loan financing, interest has to be paid on the loan. Even if the contractor finances the project from available funds, there is still a notional cost of financing, equivalent to the interest or dividends that the same funds could have earned had the contractor invested the money elsewhere (for example in investment bonds). If a project runs late, the financing period is extended, and the amount of interest or notional interest payable must increase correspondingly.

Much of the money for a large project is likely to be invested in work in progress as the project proceeds. This work in progress includes not only the tangible results of a project such as construction or manufacture, but also intangible elements such as planning and engineering or design. In many projects the contractor can only charge the customer for work that can be certified as finished. For example, in construction projects the amount of work completed usually has to be inspected and certified by an independent quality surveyor or engineer before it can be billed to the customer. The customer will not pay without the receipt of certified invoices. Certified invoices are usually linked to planned events or *milestones* or to a measured amount of work performed. If the work has not been done, a certified invoice cannot be issued. The contractor's cash income is then delayed, which means that the contractor must continue to finance the mounting costs of the project. The contractor could then suffer cash flow difficulties or even financial ruin.

Cost Penalties

Some contracts contain a penalty clause which provides the customer with the sanction of a cost penalty against the contractor for each day or week by which the contractor fails to meet the contracted delivery obligation.

The Total Cost Effect of Project Delays

All these time/cost considerations mean that delays on a project can easily cause a substantial increase in costs. It is clear that if work can be managed so that it proceeds without disruption against a sensible, achievable plan, much of the battle to control costs will have been won.

PERCEPTIONS OF PROJECT SUCCESS OR FAILURE BEYOND THE THREE PRIMARY OBJECTIVES

Most project managers are expected to complete their projects so that they satisfy the three primary objectives of time, performance and cost. These are usually the most important factors that drive the project contractor and they should align with the foremost expectations of the project owner. Most project management procedures (and this book) are directed towards achieving these goals, which could be summarized as delighting the customer while creating a commercial success for the contractor. In this context the contracting organization and the customer are both primary *stakeholders* in the project.

However, most projects have to satisfy more than two primary stakeholders. For example, a bank that has provided loan finance for a project will have a keen interest in whether the project succeeds or fails. There will always be people and organizations who, while not being principal stakeholders, nonetheless have an interest in how the outcome of a project might affect them. Subcontractors and suppliers are an example. Staff working on a project have a stake in the outcome because project success or failure can (apart from contributing to job satisfaction) have implications for their future employment and careers.

Identifying and Ranking the Stakeholders

Stakeholders are the people and organizations who affect, or will be affected by, the project. The principal stakeholders in most projects are as follows:

1. The customer or client;

2. The contractor that must perform all the project tasks, either directly or through suppliers and subcontractors;

3. The investor. For small projects the customer might be able to finance the project without external help, but larger projects often need financing support from one or more banks, or from other sources such as shareholders. In management projects and all other projects carried out internally within a company or group of companies, the company is the customer or client, and the internal department principally responsible for carrying out the work is effectively the contractor.

In some projects the initial customer purchases the project with the intention of selling it on to a third party. A common example is the property developer who commissions a new building from a contractor with the intention of selling it on (or leasing it) to occupiers. In that case the occupiers are sometimes known as the project *end-users*. Another example would be a customer that orders a batch of specially manufactured goods for selling on to retail customers. Those retail customers would also be end-users.

The range and nature of stakeholders will vary greatly from one project to another but the principle of stakeholder identification can be illustrated by an example. Suppose that a project has been proposed to redevelop a derelict urban area. This project will provide a shopping mall, offices, cinema and other leisure facilities, new roads and so on. The primary stakeholders for this project will certainly include the main project contractor and the project owner. The banks or other organizations financing the project will also have a considerable primary interest in the project's success or failure. Not least of the stakeholders are those who hold shares or have otherwise invested in participating companies that, by accepting an element of risk, stand to make a profit or loss from the project.Subcontractors, suppliers, staff, artisans and labourers can all be considered stakeholders, although these could be placed in the second rank. Intended occupiers of the shops, offices and other premises also have a stake in the project.

There are others who will be dependent on the secondary stakeholders. These are the wholesale suppliers of merchandise to be sold in the new shops, service staff such as car park attendants, shop and office workers, companies expecting to provide security, cleaning and maintenance services, and so on.

Public transport organizations must consider how the development will affect their passenger numbers: some of their existing services might need to be changed to suit the new travel patterns (and take advantage of the new business generated).

Then there are the various regulatory authorities, such as the local building inspectors, planning office and many other official organizations. These are all stakeholders whose decisions and actions can affect the project.

People living near the proposed development will benefit from the new shopping and leisure facilities but might resent the inconvenience of construction works and the prospect of increased traffic and noise when the new premises start to function. Parents might be concerned that their schoolchildren will have to cross streets that are busier and more hazardous. Motorists and other road users will be interested in how the new road layouts will affect their journeys. The new entertainments facilities will provide wider opportunities for live artistes.

This discussion could be carried on at length to identify still more stakeholders. Some will have power to influence the project, while others will be able only to voice opinions. All stakeholders might be ranked (primary, secondary, tertiary, etc.) according to the power that they can wield and the impact that the project will have on them.

BENEFITS REALIZATION

In most industrial and manufacturing projects the project owner should begin to realize the expected benefits immediately or shortly after the project is successfully finished and handed over (Phase 13 in Figure 1.2). A chemical plant, once successfully commissioned, should be capable of producing saleable product. A successful new office building should provide a pleasant working environment that can immediately improve staff satisfaction (and thus productivity). However, business change and IT projects can be different because their most significant benefits tend to be realized later in the project life history, during the first months (or even years) of the period shown as Phase 14 in Figure 1.2.

Consider, for example, a large-scale project that is intended to replace and standardize the customer service and invoicing systems of all the companies in an international group. The execution phase of the project is finished when the IT designers have developed, documented and tested the software. If the IT was contracted out, the IT specialist contractor might have had a successful project outcome, with all three primary objectives of cost, performance and time satisfied at the time of hand over to the user company. However, there is much more to the success of a management change project than the technical excellence and performance of the IT. It is only when the new system is up, running and accepted by the managers and staff of all the companies in the group that the project owner can begin to regard the project as a success. Implementing new systems and procedures can be very difficult in any organization where the staff resist change, have understandable concerns about possible redundancies, come from a rich mix of different cultures, or resent having to cope with all the teething problems that significant changes create.

In recent years these difficulties have led to new ways of assessing and managing the benefits realization of management change and IT projects. It is now recognized that the benefits realization process should start during early project definition by establishing benchmarks that can be put in place in the business plan. These benchmarks have some similarity with the milestones set in the project execution plans of all projects, but for management change and IT projects there are two important differences:

1. The most important benchmarks often occur some time after initial handover and commissioning of the project from the contractor to the customer (remembering that the contractor and owner can be in the same company).
2. Each benchmark must be *directly* associated with a cash inflow, cost saving or other real benefit that can be tracked to a favourable entry in the company's accounts or management reports.

Benefits realization is appreciated among the more enlightened management fraternity as the most important driver in a management change or IT project, so that the intended long-term benefits are kept in the minds of the project manager and the other project stakeholders. There is no reason why the perception of benefits realization should not apply to industrial and manufacturing projects.

PRINCIPAL ORGANIZATIONS REPRESENTING THE PROJECT MANAGEMENT PROFESSION

Both of the following organizations offer different membership grades and certification schemes for project professionals. Both arrange seminars and produce or promote publications.

The International Association of Project Management (IPMA)

The profession of project management is represented by the International Association of Project Management (IPMA). The corporate member of the IPMA in the UK is The Association for Project Management (APM) and further information about them is available from their secretariat at:

> The Association for Project Management,
> Ibis House,
> Regent Park,
> Summerleys Road
> Princes Risborough,
> Buckinghamshire,
> HP27 9LE
> United Kingdom
> Telephone: 0845 458 1944
> Fax: 0845 458 8807
> Email: info@apm.org.uk
> Website: apm.org.uk

The Project Management Institute (PMI)

With its headquarters in the US and chapters in many countries the PMI is the world's largest professional project management organization. For more information, contact PMI at:

> PMI Headquarters,
> Four Campus Boulevard,
> Newtown Square,
> PA 19073-3299,
> USA
> Telephone: +610-356-4600
> Email: pmihq@pmi.org
> Website: www.pmi.org

REFERENCES

Hartman, F.T. (2000), *Don't Park Your Brain Outside*, Newtown Square, PA, Project Management Institute.

Morris, Peter W.G. (1994), *The Management of Projects*, London, Thomas Telford.

2 *Defining the Project Task*

Every project should be defined as accurately and fully as possible before it is allowed to start. The investor must know how the money will be spent and what benefits can be expected in return, the contractors must know the extent of their commitments before the contract is agreed. Figure 2.1 illustrates that project definition is a continuous process, beginning before a project can be authorized and not ending until the project has been completed, when its final as-built state can be recorded.

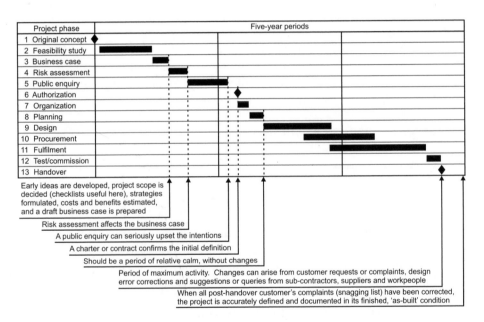

2.1 Definition of a large project from initial concept to completion

PROJECTS WHICH ARE IMPOSSIBLE TO DEFINE ACCURATELY

Although this chapter is about defining a project, a few proposed projects are so surrounded by uncertainty that they cannot be defined adequately before work starts. If an investor still wishes to proceed with such a project, there are safeguards that can limit the exposure to risk.

Limiting the Risk in Projects that Cannot be Defined at Birth

Stage-gating

Projects for pure scientific research are an extreme case of initial uncertainty. Chapter 1 mentioned how a step-by-step or 'stage-gating' approach can be used to authorize such projects, releasing resources in controlled amounts so that the risks can be kept within defined bounds. Each new tranche of investment will depend on the satisfactory outcome of a periodical project review. If the outlook is not good, the plug can be pulled on the project and all further expenditure stopped.

Stage-gating is a valuable method for the damage limitation of any project that cannot be defined with certainty in its early days. However, people working in a stage-gated project are unlikely to be well motivated because they work under the constant threat of sudden project closure. If the employer cannot guarantee equivalent alternative employment on other projects, some staff might decide to end the uncertainty by seeking safer employment elsewhere.

Avoidance of fixed-price contracts

A commercial contractor whose role in a project has not been clearly defined can accept the order with some confidence if the payment arrangements, instead of being fixed-price, guarantee reimbursement of the contractor's costs plus reasonable fees or mark-ups for profit. Such reimbursable project terms should ensure that the customer or investor bears all the financial risk. But even with the promise of full cost reimbursement, poor project definition can still cause difficulties for the contactor. It is always inconvenient to commit resources to a project whose duration is unknown and which is liable to be cancelled at short notice.

Provisional cost items in fixed-price contracts

Understandably, contractors are unwilling to quote fixed prices for projects that cannot be fully and accurately defined before work begins. On the other hand, customers generally prefer to sign contracts where the prices are fixed, so that they know the extent of their commitments and can set their own budget limits with confidence.

Contractors (particularly for construction projects) often deal with this difficulty by listing and cost-estimating separately any parts of the project that cannot adequately be defined before work starts. These unknown or high-risk items are listed as provisional cost items (or pc sums) and are excluded from the work quoted in the fixed price. Here is an example. Consider a project to refurbish a building where part of the internal roof structure is hidden from view and there is no access for inspection by a surveyor. When the contractor submits a fixed-price proposal for this refurbishment project, a provisional cost item would be appended estimating the additional charges that would be incurred by the customer should wood rot or beetle infestation be found when the roof timbers are uncovered.

Feasibility studies to improve early project definition

The investor faced with an uncertain outlook for a large project might start by commissioning a feasibility study from a consultant or consulting company to obtain more facts and expert advice. This approach is often used to appraise the technical, logistical, environmental, commercial and financial aspects of all kinds of projects that require a high level of investment.

A feasibility study for a large capital project can take years to prepare and cost millions of pounds. But a good feasibility study report can recommend the most effective project strategy and define the risks, as well as stating the achievable objectives and predicting the costs and resulting benefits realization.

Banks and other institutions asked to finance or guarantee large projects might want to see a satisfactory feasibility study report before agreeing to provide finance.

Government departments usually carry out or commission feasibility study reports for projects that are of significant importance. Two examples at the time of writing are Britain's proposed High Speed Rail Project (HS2) and competing schemes for expanding London's airport capacity.

CHECKLISTS

Checklists are a good way of ensuring that no important task or cost item is forgotten when a new project is being evaluated. Contractors with good experience in their particular field of operation can develop comprehensive checklists for use when compiling project cost estimates and proposals.

Checklist Examples

Routine sales

One very simple application of a project definition checklist is seen when a sales engineer takes a customer's order for equipment that is standard, but which can be ordered with a range of options. The sales engineer might use a standard pro forma (either on a pad or a computer), entering data in boxes and ticking off the options that the customer requires. People selling replacement windows use such methods. So do salesmen in automobile showrooms. Standard formats are convenient and help to ensure that no important detail is forgotten when the order is taken and passed back to the factory or warehouse for action.

Construction projects

Companies about to tender for large civil engineering, construction, petrochemical or mining projects can make good use of checklists. A suitable checklist might be used to ensure that all aspects of the building and performance of a new chemical plant are considered. Another case would be to ensure that the accommodation space and standards in a new building can be appropriately specified. Local climatic and geological data at an overseas construction site may have to be defined.

The designer or contractor of a construction project may not be aware of hazards such as high winds, potential earth tremors or flooding. It is also necessary to check whether or not any special statutory regulations apply in the region, particularly in unfamiliar territory overseas. Other data might cover national working practices and the influence of local trade unions, the availability of suitable local labour, facilities to be provided for the contractor's expatriate staff and so on. Checklists are ideal in these circumstances. The example in Figure 2.2 includes items that might feature in a checklist for a project that involves civil engineering, mining or construction at a distant site.

Management change and IT projects

Internal management change projects can consume prodigious amounts of time, money and other resources but cause considerable harm to staff morale and the company's operations if they fail. Inadequate project definition can be the root cause of such disasters and, here again, checklists are invaluable. But there is a big difficulty in compiling checklists for management change projects when compared with other projects. Organizations undertaking large internal change projects will probably do so very infrequently, perhaps even only once in ten years or less. Companies intending to make changes to their internal organization, procedures and IT do not have the experience of past projects that is essential for compiling checklists. This is where the employment of a competent consultant can be very beneficial.

Consultancy companies with relevant experience from their work with many past and present clients are able to give advice and help to define this kind of project. These companies do have the necessary experience from which to compile checklists. A checklist compiled by one consulting company (Isochron Limited) is shown in Figure 2.3.

Project site and other local conditions

Availability of utilities
- Electrical power
- Potable water
- Other water
- Sewerage
- Other services

Transport
- Existing roads: Access difficulties (low bridges, weight limits, etc.)
- Nearest railpoint
- Nearest suitable seaport
- Nearest commercial airport
- Local airstrip
- Local transport and insurance arrangements

Physical conditions
- Seismic situation
- Temperature range
- Rainfall or other precipitation
- Humidity
- Wind force and direction
- Dust
- Barometric pressure
- Site plans and survey
- Soil investigation and foundation requirements

Local workshop and manufacturing facilities

Local sources of bulk materials

Local plant hire

Site safety and security

Local human resources available
- Professional
- Skilled
- Unskilled

Site accommodation arrangements for:
- Offices
- Secure stores

Site living accommodation for:
- Expatriate managers and engineers
- Artisans
- Short stay visitors
- Married quarters (see separate checklist if these are required)

Other site facilities
- First aid, medical and hospital facilities
- Catering and messing arrangements
- Hotels or other accommodation for VIPs
- Local banking arrangements

Communications
- General mail and airmail service
- Special mail or courier service
- Telephone over public network
- Telephone over dedicated terrestrial or satellite link
- Fax
- E-mail
- Other

Contractual and commercial conditions

How firm are the proposals?
What are the client's relative priorities for:
- Time?
- Cost?
- Quality?
What are the client's delivery requirements?
Do we know the client's budget levels?
Scope of work envisaged:
- Basic design only?
- Fully detailed design?
- Procurement responsibility: (ourselves, the client, or someone else?)
- Construction responsibility: (ourselves, the client or a contractor?)
- Commissioning, training, operating and maintenance manuals, etc.
How accurate are the existing cost estimates:
- Ball park?
- Comparative?
- Have all estimates been checked against the estimating manual checklists?
How is the project to be financed?
Is there to be a financial guarantor?
What do we know about the client's financial status and payment record?
Are contract penalty clauses expected?
Is the pricing to be firm or other?
What are the likely arrangements for stage or progress payments?
What retention payment will be imposed?
What insurances must we arrange?
What guarantees or warranties will the client expect?

2.2 Part of a definition checklist for a mining project

010000	**Business analysis**
010100	Business redesign
010101	Major process procedures design
010102	IS procedures design
010103	Data model design (logical)
010104	Report and management information design
010105	Develop procedures documentation
010200	Current state assessment
010201	Information systems review
010202	Use organization assessment
010203	Process assessment
010204	Reporting and MI assessment
020000	**Business change**
020100	Business user training
020101	Identify communities to be trained
020102	Conduct training needs analysis
020103	Develop training plan
020104	Develop training course material
020105	Schedule training events
020106	Administer training events
020107	Deliver training courses
020108	Monitor training feedback
020200	Communications
020201	Identify communication audiences
020202	Develop communication strategy
020203	Select communication media
020204	Develop communication plan
020205	Implement communication plan
020206	Assess audience understanding of key message
020207	Update communication plan
020300	Project contract development
020301	Identify objectives
020302	Identify event milestones
020303	Identify business values
020304	Match flashpoints to value drivers
020305	Quantify values
020306	Determine project cost
020307	Balance value against cost
020308	Develop project contract
020309	Obtain approval

2.3   Initial task checklist for a management change project

DEFINING THE PROJECT SCOPE

Before signing a contract it is essential that the contractor knows exactly what the customer expects to receive in return for money spent on the project. The project specification should set out all the requirements clearly, so that they can be understood and similarly interpreted by customer and contractor alike.

Particularly important is defining the way in which responsibility for the work is to be shared between the contractor, the customer, and others. The scope of work required from the contractor (the size of the contractor's contribution to the project) must be made clear. At its simplest, the scope of work required might be limited to making and delivering a piece of hardware in accordance with drawings supplied by the customer. At the other extreme, the scope of a large construction or process plant project could be defined so that the contractor handles the project entirely, and is responsible for all work until the purchaser is able to accept delivery or handover of a fully completed and proven project (known as a *turnkey operation*).

Whether the scope of work lies at one of these extremes or the other, there is almost always a range of ancillary items that have to be considered. Will the contractor be responsible for training customer's staff and, if so, how much (if any) of this training is to be included in the project contract and price? What about commissioning, or support during the first few weeks or months of the project's working life? What sort of warranty or guarantee is going to be expected? Are any operating or maintenance instructions to be provided? If so how many copies and in what language?

Answers to all of these questions must be provided as part of the project task definition before cost estimates, tenders and binding contracts can be completed.

THE CONTRACTOR'S STRATEGY

When a project contractor evaluates a proposed new project, an important aspect of definition is the intended strategy for performing the work. Suppose that, after consideration of a customer's enquiry, a contractor decides to prepare a fixed-price tender. The contractor must develop and record an intended strategy for designing and carrying out the work. Without a good understanding of the project requirements and the intended strategy for meeting those requirements, estimating, budgeting and pricing become very uncertain, even impossible processes.

Without a documented internal project specification for design and strategy, there would be a danger that a project could be costed, priced and sold against one design and strategic intention but executed using a different, more costly, approach. This risk increases when there is a long delay between submitting the tender to the potential customer and actually receiving the order.

Not Invented Here

It sometimes happens that engineers prefer to create a new design even though a perfectly adequate design already exists. They feel that they could do better themselves, or find fault unreasonably with the designs of others (even though those other engineers might enjoy a good reputation and their designs have been proven in successful earlier projects). This state of affairs is sometimes called the 'not invented here' syndrome. The results can be ugly. Two of many examples from my own experience follow; names have been omitted to avoid any risk of subsequent unpleasantness.

Case 1

A British company won an important export order to design, supply and install specially built electronic patient monitoring equipment for the operating theatres of a European university teaching hospital. Following internal company reorganization, the project's chief engineer resigned. His successor had different ideas and caused all design work completed or in progress to be scrapped and restarted. The design costs alone of that project eventually reached the same figure as the fixed price for which the whole project had originally been sold. That meant that the company had to write off the original design costs and bear all the considerable manufacturing and installation costs of the project itself. The project was delivered very late.

Case 2

An American company with a very high reputation for product excellence sent a set of engineering and manufacturing drawings to its new British subsidiary. This was a complete, finished design package for a large heavy engineering project. The intention was that it would provide the brand new machining and assembly shops with work during the start-up period when the local British design team was becoming established. The drawings produced in America required 'Anglicizing', which meant that the British engineers had to check all the drawings and, with help from the new purchasing department, ensure that the standards specifications and lists of bought-out components would be suitable for purchase from British suppliers.

What happened was that the UK team poured scorn on the American design, and the whole project was redesigned from scratch at a cost of several million pounds.

Construction Specification

Construction projects offer another example of work that has to be defined by specification. All building contractors of any repute work from detailed specifications. The requirement to satisfy the statutory authorities is just one reason for documenting specifications of building location, layout, intended use, means of escape in case of fire, appearance, and many other factors.

There are, of course, many design aspects of a building which can greatly affect its costs, including for instance the style of interior decoration, the quality of the fittings and installed equipment, lighting and air conditioning standards.

Disputes can be minimized, if not prevented altogether, when a contractor produces a detailed project specification and asks the customer to accept it before the contract is signed. Any changes subsequently requested by the customer can then be identified easily as changes from the agreed specification and charged as variations to the original order.

SPECIFICATIONS FOR INTERNALLY FUNDED DEVELOPMENT PROJECTS

Development programmes aimed at introducing additions or changes to a company's product range are prone to overspending on cost budgets and late completion. One cause of this phenomenon is that chronic engineer's disease, which I used to call 'creeping improvement sickness'. Now people call this 'scope creep'. All projects are prone to scope creep. An imaginary case example follows that illustrates this danger.

The Bikes 'n' Skates Project

Bikes 'n' Skates plc, a company producing bicycles and other wheeled devices, decided to add a children's motorized scooter to its product range. The aim was to produce a colourful two-wheeled affair with a foot platform and simple front column steering. That is the traditional scooter design with which we are all familiar from our childhood days, but now a small petrol motor would drive the rear wheel. A simple brake on the front wheel would help prevent accidents to riders, pedestrians and property.

Fierce competition from cheap foreign imports did not allow Bikes 'n' Skates to set high prices, although the company could charge a premium price because of its good reputation for making attractive, reliable, safe and high-quality products.

The scooter project was started in January, at the start of a new year, with the intention of having scooters in the warehouse for distribution and sale during the next Christmas season. The product was to be advertised in the run up to Christmas (which in the UK begins in July or August). In addition, models were to be exhibited and demonstrated at an autumn toy trade fair.

Management confidence was high. They had commissioned market research and the reports were favourable. The company had all the resources to do this job. By any standards this was a simple, small project that needed only simple budgeting and project control: it was not dependent for its success on state-of-the-art project management techniques. Everything should have been straightforward. There was nothing that could go wrong. Or was there?

The kick-off meeting

The launch of the new scooter design started with a meeting in the chief engineer's office. In addition to the chief engineer the meeting included representatives from other involved departments, such as sales, purchasing and manufacturing. The other essential person at this meeting was the responsible design engineer (George).

Discussion was focused on setting George on the right track to create the scooter envisaged by the company's directors. Thus George was given a set task with a number of objectives. However, these objectives were fairly broadly based and they were not written into a formal specification.

George emerged from the meeting full of ideas arising from the discussion and carrying his own notes and sketches. He was given some idea of target production costs, styling, performance, the preferred selling price and a date for stocks to be available in the warehouse for distribution and release to the market. He looked forward with excitement to testing the prototype himself, in the company car park. His kids could test it too.

Initial design

George was bubbling over with enthusiasm. Most competent engineers become keen when given responsibility for a new project on which their creative abilities can be unleashed. After a few weeks' activity involving George and the company's prototype model workshop, George was able to wheel out the first experimental model of the new scooter. This model was subjected to test rides, reliability and safety tests and the critical attention of various experts. Among the witnesses were marketing staff, an industrial styling designer and production engineers from the factory departments that were going to manufacture the scooter.

Preproduction stage

Following successful evaluation of the prototype, the next stage in the project was the preparation of production drawings, parts lists and specifications from which the first batch of scooters could be manufactured and tested. As expected, this phase of the project took longer than the few weeks needed to build the first trial model. The production department decided to go ahead with tooling, and the production engineers and others began to plan for full-scale manufacture.

Second thoughts

Apart from having to answer occasional production or purchasing queries, George had to endure a period of waiting. He became bored. His active mind was starved of work. This caused him to reflect on his design and led him to some second thoughts. On thumbing through the engine supplier's catalogue he found that he could have specified a better petrol engine, capable of propelling a heavier, older rider and giving more power in reserve. An informal telephone call to the supplier revealed that the order for engines could be changed without cancellation charges. So George, not a faint-hearted person afraid to make decisions, told the supplier to change the order. Then, almost as an afterthought, George asked Bikes 'n' Skates's astonished purchasing manager to issue a purchase order amendment for the new engines, mentioning that these would cost 15 per cent more than the smaller original engines and take three weeks longer to obtain.

Early modifications

George had to redesign the scooter chassis to provide stronger fixings for the new engine at a stage when the trial production batch had just started. Only simple changes were needed, but the first trial batch (work-in-progress) had to be scrapped. Modified drawings and parts lists were issued to the production and purchasing departments. This change caused a three-week hold-up in the programme.

Unforeseen problems

At length, and in spite of the delays and additional expense, the prototype batch was completed and passed back to George and others for evaluation. George was dismayed to find that, because the enhanced engine power had increased the maximum speed from five to eight miles per hour, the braking system was no longer adequate. It was indeed unsafe. That left George with the following two choices:

1. Revert to the initial design, using the original engine and chassis.
2. Modify the brake design.

George, a person of high principles, could not contemplate the first choice because the idea of degrading the performance did not appeal to him. He considered redesign and changes to the brake manufacture a small price to pay in return for the improved performance. Accordingly George made and issued new drawings for the brake components and assembly.

Once again the manufacturing department had to be told to stop work and cancel a batch of components. George produced the revised drawings as quickly as he could, but the project was delayed by four more weeks. However, the modified prototype scooters eventually passed all their tests, so that tooling and planning for full-scale production could begin. All design and performance characteristics of the scooter were now excellent, exceeding those envisaged by the marketing department.

A good result?

The resulting scooters were unquestionably very good. When the production line started the Bikes 'n' Skates staff knew that they were making high-performance scooters. George was well pleased with the results of his labours and congratulated himself on a job well done.

The company's management was not so well pleased. The oft-repeated phrase 'time is money' is as true in project management as anywhere, and it is usually safe to assume that if the planned timescale has been exceeded, so have the budgeted costs. Development costs for this small scooter project rocketed over budget. Not only did it cost more to design the scooter than intended, but also the manufacturing costs had become so high that the intended profit margin was severely reduced. The first batch of scooters was produced so late that only a preproduction model could be exhibited at the autumn trade fair, and there were no warehouse stocks from which to supply the Christmas orders.

This disaster could have been prevented if George had carried out his original instructions. But what exactly were those original instructions? George was given only vague verbal guidelines at the start of this project and it was easy for him to choose and change his own course of action. This simple example illustrates some of the pitfalls that can happen in a project that has no adequate project specification.

George did, in fact, design a very good product, but not the product that management expected. He allowed his own ideas to intrude and he lost sight of the original objectives. George fell into a common trap by allowing the *best* to become the enemy of the *good*.

All of these problems could have been avoided if the following steps had been taken:

1. The project should have been launched with a written specification.
2. A more effective check could have been kept on progress if a simple programme schedule (such as a bar chart) had used and included as part of the project specification.
3. No change should have been allowed without formal approval from higher management. Procedures for controlling changes are given in Chapter 11. It is enough here to note that the unauthorized changes would not have been allowed under closer management control.

George would have been kept on the right lines by the provision of a formal product specification and development programme, by the sensible control of modifications and, of course, by the-day-to day supervision of his superiors.

THE PROJECT SPECIFICATION AND VERSION CONTROL

Given the importance of specifying project requirements as accurately as possible, it is appropriate to end this chapter with some thoughts on the specification document.

Although customers might be clear from the very first about their needs, it is usual for dialogue to take place between a customer and one or more potential contractors before a contract for any project of significant size is signed. During these discussions, each competing contractor can be expected to make various preliminary proposals to the customer for executing the project. Some of those proposals might suggest changes to the customer's initial enquiry specification – changes intended to improve the project deliverables or otherwise work to the mutual benefit of both customer and contractor. In some engineering companies this pre-project phase is aptly known as *solution engineering*.

For some projects a practice known as simultaneous engineering can be used. Here the contractor's engineering group works with the customer's own engineers to produce and recommend an engineering solution which they consider would best suit the customer and yet be practical for the contractor to build. Solution engineering might last a few days, several months, or even years. It can be an expensive undertaking, especially when the resulting tender fails to win the contract.

Although it is tempting to imagine the chosen contractor's engineers settling down contentedly to write a single, definitive project specification, the practice is likely to be quite different. The first draft descriptive text, written fairly early in the proceedings, will probably undergo various additions and amendments as the outline solution develops. It is likely to be revised and reissued more than once. The text will typically be associated with a pile of drawings, artists' impressions, flowsheets, schedules, or other documents appropriate to the type of project. Accordingly all the documentation might suffer several changes and re-issues before the preferred solution is reached.

Projects of all types can undergo a process of early discussion and changes before a contract is made. For example, the requirements for a management change or IT project are likely to evolve as the various stakeholders make their views known, until a final consensus definition of the project task is reached.

So, as all these discussions take place, the original draft project specification can undergo a series of changes (usually while still keeping to the original objectives). So a number of different design and strategy solutions can often exist by the time a contract is signed.

A vital requirement when a contract is eventually signed, or a charter is approved for a management change project, is to be able to refer without ambiguity to the correct version of the project specification. The correct version is that which defines the project according to the finally agreed intentions. The process of ensuring this is sometimes known as version control. Remember that the *latest* issue of any document might not be the *correct* issue as finally agreed.

The only safe way to identify any document is to label it with a unique serial or identifying number, and augment that with a revision number every time the document is re-issued with changes. If there are drawings and other documents that cannot be bound in with the specification document, these attachments must be listed on a contents sheet that is bound into the specification, and the list must give the correct serial and revision number of every such document.

Then everyone can be reasonably confident that the project has been defined.

3 Estimating the Project Costs

The obvious reason for estimating costs is for pricing commercial and industrial projects. But good cost estimates are vital for every project that needs budgetary cost control – which for practical purposes should mean *all* projects.

COST ELEMENTS

Project managers and every cost estimator and cost engineer should have some knowledge of the terms used by cost accountants in general and of their company's cost accounting department in particular. Figure 3.1 shows the principal elements of a typical cost estimate. There are important distinctions between direct and indirect costs.

- *Direct costs* can be directly and wholly attributed to the project and are the costs of labour and materials needed to perform the project tasks. Direct costs are also called *variable costs*, because they vary with the rate at which project work is performed. When no project work is done, no direct costs are incurred. Direct costs are expected to add value to the project.
- *Indirect costs* are the overhead costs of running the business. People often refer to these costs simply as overheads. They include items such as heating, lighting, rent, council rates and property maintenance. The salaries of management, accountants, salespeople, the HR department and all other people in administration jobs are usually also indirect costs. Most indirect costs continue relentlessly whether any project work is done or not, and tend not to vary much from one day to the next. Thus indirect costs are also *fixed costs*. Indirect costs add cost to a project without adding value.

Figure 3.1 also shows that cost items can be either 'above the line' or 'below the line'. Above the line costs include the total estimated direct costs plus a pro rata allowance for overheads. Below the line items are usually allowances intended to give some protection from risk and ensure that the project will be profitable.

Above-the-line items	Direct (variable) costs	Direct labour	The wages and salaries for labour time that can be directly attributed to the project. Usually costed at standard cost rates applicable to each staff grade.
		Direct materials	Equipment, materials and bought-out services used specifically on the project.
		Direct expenses	Travel, accommodation and other costs chargeable specifically to the project. Can include the hiring of external consultants.
	Indirect (fixed) costs	Overhead costs	The general costs of running the business, such as general management and accommodation. Usually calculated as a proportion of total direct costs. Not usually applicable if the project is itself charged as an overhead.
Below-the-line items		Contingency sum	An addition, usually calculated as a small percentage of the total above-the-line costs, in an attempt to compensate for estimating errors and omissions, unfunded project changes and other unexpected costs.
		Escalation	An allowance for costs that increase with time with annual cost inflation. Important for long-duration projects when national cost inflation rates are high.
		Mark-up for profit	These two items apply to projects sold to external clients. There are various ways in which they can be calculated. They are often set according to the strength of the competition and what the market will stand. These are management decisions (not part of the cost estimating process) but such decisions are always made easier when there is confidence in the cost estimating accuracy.
		Selling price	
		Provisional sums	The estimated costs of items not included in the quoted price which might have to be charged extra if the need for them is subsequentlyrevealed

3.1   Elements of a cost estimate for a typical industrial project

ACCURACY OF COST ESTIMATES

Good project definition should minimize cost estimating errors but these can never be eliminated. Estimates are usually only best guesses. Thus initial cost estimates can never be perfectly accurate and most projects will produce some unwelcome surprises that could lead to budget overspends (*variances*). The estimator's task is to use all the data and time available to produce the best estimate possible: that is, a carefully calculated judgement of what the project should cost if all goes according to plan.

Accurate estimates improve the effectiveness of cost budgets and resource schedules. They also help when making project pricing decisions where competition forces management to work with small profit margins.

Classification of Estimates According to Confidence

Apart from the estimator's skill, accuracy depends on good project definition and sufficient time for preparing the estimates. Some companies classify cost estimates according to the degree of confidence that can be placed in them. Here are examples used by one company:

- *Ballpark estimates* are made when only rough outline information exists or when there is no time to prepare a detailed estimate. A ballpark estimate might achieve an accuracy of ±25 per cent, given a generous amount of luck and good judgement.
- *Comparative estimates* are made by comparing work to be done on a new project with similar work done in the past. These estimates can usually be attempted before detailed design and without final materials lists or work schedules but a detailed project specification is essential. It should be possible to achieve ±15 per cent accuracy. Comparative estimates are often used when tendering for new work.
- *Feasibility estimates* need a significant amount of preliminary project design. In construction projects the building specification, site data, provisional layouts and drawings for services are all necessary. Quotations must be obtained from the potential suppliers of expensive project equipment or subcontracts. Material take-offs or other schedules should be available for estimating the costs of materials. Feasibility estimates should be accurate to better than ±10 per cent and they are often used for construction project tenders.
- *Definitive estimates* cannot be made until much of the work has been done. They are a combination of costs actually incurred plus an estimate of costs remaining to project completion. Estimates become definitive when accuracy improves to better than ±5 per cent.

Organizations will use different names and accuracy limits for their cost estimates. It is also possible to find asymmetric limits, so that a company might, for example, assume that its ballpark estimates are accurate to within plus 50 or minus 10 per cent. Clearly project managers must be aware of the methods used in their companies.

STANDARD ESTIMATING TABLES

Standard tables (based on rates per quantities of work or materials) exist to help the estimator in projects such as construction and civil engineering. Spon Press (an imprint of the Taylor and Francis publishing group) produces books of such tables and updates them annually. Companies can sometimes develop their own tables as they gain experience. However, for many projects cost estimating remains a matter of personal skill and judgement.

COMPILING THE TASK LIST

Cost estimating begins by making a 'shopping list' of all the tasks and materials that are going to cost money. Compilation of this list can be difficult but clearly the omission of any significant item will result in an underestimate for the project. A work breakdown (described in Chapter 6) is a logical way of considering the total project and its elements and can reduce errors of omission. But at the outset of a project it is most likely that the work breakdown has to be compiled in fairly broad terms, because much of the detail will not be known until the project has advanced well into its design phase.

Software Tasks

Software is a familiar term in the context of IT, but most industrial and commercial projects have software in the form of schedules for inspection and testing, instruction and maintenance manuals, lists of recommended spares and consumables and so forth. These software tasks must usually be allowed for and included in the task list and project cost estimates.

Forgotten Tasks

Tasks often forgotten for manufacturing projects include processes such as protective coatings, heat treatments, silk-screen printing, engraving, inspection and testing. In some firms these may be included in overhead costs, but in many others they will not. For construction projects there can be many easily forgotten expenses, such as the provision of site huts, rubbish skips and so on.

An expensive item sometimes neglected during cost estimating is the work of final commissioning, handover and customer acceptance of the completed project.

Contracts often demand that the contractor provides training facilities for some of the customer's operatives or technicians. Training sessions can involve the contractor's senior engineers and technicians in much hard work, both in the actual training and in preparing the training material beforehand.

DOCUMENTING THE COST ESTIMATES

Estimates should be set out according to a standard company procedure, itemized where possible by cost codes within the work breakdown structure. This will help to ensure that comparisons can readily be made later between the estimates and the cost accountant's records of the actual costs incurred, on a strict item-for-item basis. This is an essential part of cost control. As experience and data build up over a few years, it will also contribute to the accuracy of comparative estimates for new projects. If no work breakdown structure exists, the task list should still be sectioned and arranged as logically as possible.

Standard Estimate Formats

Calculations performed in odd corners of notebooks, on scraps of paper, and on the backs (or even fronts) of envelopes are prone to error and premature loss. Cost estimates should be tabulated and recorded in a logical and consistent manner, for which standard estimating formats can help considerably (either as hard copy or as computer files).

Project estimating forms (spreadsheets) can be collated to fit the kind of work breakdown structures described in Chapter 6. One sheet can be allocated to each main project work package or group of tasks. Every row on the forms can be allocated to one task so that adding the costs along each row gives a task cost estimate. Totalling relevant columns provides a basis for compiling department budgets and coarse aggregated resource schedules.

COST ESTIMATE			Project number and title or sales reference:						Estimate number: Case: Date:				
Estimate for:			Compiled by:						Page of				
1	2	3	4	5	6	7	8	9	10	11	12	13	14	15
Code	Item	Qty	Labour times and costs by department or standard grade						Total direct labour cost	Overhead cost at %	Materials			Total cost 10+11 +12+13
			Hrs	£	Hrs	£	Hrs	£	Hrs	£	Hrs	£	Hrs	£			Standard or net cost	Burden %	Longest delivery (weeks)	

3.2 A general purpose estimating form, particularly applicable to manufacturing projects

Figure 3.2 shows an example of a general purpose estimating format. This version allows six different grades of labour to be shown and assumes that all man-hours will be costed at the appropriate standard cost rates. The standard grade code and rate used can be entered in the space at the head of each labour column.

There is no need to complicate a general purpose estimating form by adding extra columns for such things as special tooling or heat treatments. These items can be designated as tasks, so that they can be written along rows in same way as any other task.

The column headed 'longest lead time' in the materials section, although not connected directly with cost estimating, is convenient because the people who estimate material costs using this format are the people most likely to be able to say what delivery times can be expected. Inclusion of these lead times can help later, when planning the project timescale.

COLLECTING DEPARTMENTAL ESTIMATES

Networked computers provide a method for gathering and collating information from a number of different sources, which is of course a requirement in cost estimating. Some project management software, although designed originally for planning and control, allows system users to add estimating data to the project database. However, these methods are passive, and rely on the goodwill of people to provide the data.

Estimating expects people to make commitments and difficult judgements. Thus it is often regarded as a chore to be avoided if possible. A firm approach is sometimes needed to extract estimates from reluctant supervisors and managers. Personal canvassing can produce quick and dependable results. The process starts by preparing a list of all known project tasks, arranged in logical subsets according to the work breakdown structure. The project manager or delegate can then tour all the departments involved, installing himself purposefully at each relevant manager's desk and remaining firmly rooted there until all the desired cost estimates have been extracted.

Canvassing also gives an opportunity to assess the estimating capabilities of the individuals concerned. Any estimate which appears unrealistic or outrageous can be questioned on the spot, and other queries can be sorted out with the least possible fuss and delay. One type of question which must frequently be asked is 'Here is a job said to require four man-weeks; can four men do it in one week, or must the job be spread over four weeks with only one person able to work on it?' Answers to such questions will be needed later for scheduling resources.

Cost Estimating Units

Generally speaking, while wages and their related standard cost rates change from year to year, the time needed to carry out any particular job by a given method will not. Man-hours are therefore regarded as a more constant basis than original costs for making new labour estimates. Comparative estimates for labour made by scanning the cost records from past projects should thus be based initially on man-hours, man-weeks or other suitable time units. Once the new work times have been estimated, current cost rates can be applied to produce the new project's cost estimates.

THE ESTIMATING ABILITIES OF DIFFERENT PEOPLE

Project cost estimating, particularly for labour times, is not an exact science. If ten people were to be asked separately to judge the time needed for a particular project task, it is inconceivable that ten identical answers would be received. Repeat this exercise with the same group of people for a number of different project tasks, and it is likely that a pattern will emerge when the results are analysed. Some of those people will tend always to estimate on the low side. Others might give answers that are consistently high. The person collecting project cost estimates needs to be aware of this problem. In fact, just as it is possible to classify estimates according to confidence in their accuracy, so it is possible to classify the estimators themselves.

Optimistic Estimators

It can be assumed that estimates will more frequently be understated than overstated. Many people seem to be blessed with an unquenchable spirit of optimism when asked to predict completion times for any specific task. 'I can polish off that little job in three days,' it is often claimed, but three weeks later the only things produced are excuses. Without such optimism the world might be a much duller place in which to live and work, but the project manager's life would be far easier.

An interesting feature of optimistic estimators is the way in which they allow their Cloud-cuckoo-land dreams to persist, even after seeing several jobs completed in double the time that they originally forecast. They continue to make estimates which are every bit as hopeful as the last, and appear quite unable to learn from experience. Engineers and designers are perhaps the chief offenders in this respect. Fortunately such estimators are at least consistent in their trend. Shrewd project managers will learn from experience just how pronounced this trend is in their own company. Better still, they will be able to assign error correction factors to particular individuals. It is often necessary to add about 50 per cent to the original estimates to counteract the original optimism.

Pessimistic Estimators

Occasionally another kind of individual is encountered who, unlike the more usual optimist, can be relied upon to overestimate most tasks. Pessimism is not particularly common and, when seen, it might pay to investigate the underlying cause. Possibly the estimator lacks experience or is incompetent, but incompetence tends to produce random results, and not a consistent error bias. The picture becomes clearer, if more unsavoury, when it is remembered that project estimates play a large part in determining total departmental budgets. High (pessimistic) estimates could produce bigger manpower budgets, leading to enlarged departments and thus higher status of the departmental heads. In these cases, therefore, 'E' stands not only for 'estimator' but also for 'empire builder'. Correction factors are possible, but action is more effective when it is aimed not at the estimates but at the estimators.

Inconsistent Estimators

The inconsistent estimator is the bane of the project manager's existence. Here we find a person who is seemingly incapable of estimating any job at all, giving answers that range over the whole spectrum from ridiculous pessimism to ludicrous optimism. The only characteristic consistently displayed is, in fact, inconsistency. The estimator's incompetence or inexperience suggest themselves as the most likely causes. Complacency could be another cause. People looking forward to retirement rather than promotion, and staff with a laissez-faire attitude to work can display these symptoms.

Unfortunately this category can manifest itself even at departmental head level, the very people most frequently asked to provide estimates. Only time can solve this one.

Accurate Estimators

There is a possibility of finding a person capable of providing estimates that prove to be consistently accurate. This possibility is so remote that it can almost be discounted. When this rare phenomenon does occur it can unsettle a work-hardened project manager who has, through long experience, learned that it pays to question every report received and never to take any estimate at its face value.

Correction Factors

Why not try to educate the estimators until they all produce accurate estimates and lose their characteristic errors? Prevention is, after all, better than cure. But the results of such a re-education programme must be unpredictable, with the effects varying from person to person, upsetting the previous steady state. In any case, all the estimators could be expected to slip back into their old ways eventually and, during the process, their estimating bias could lie anywhere on the scale between extreme optimism and pessimism. Arguing wastes time if nothing is achieved. Why not accept the situation as it exists and be grateful that it is at least predictable?

Here, then, is a picture of a person who has obtained a set of cost estimates for a project, sitting down with a list of all the estimators who were involved, complete with the correction factor deemed appropriate for each individual, and then factoring each estimate accordingly. Far-fetched? This procedure has been proved in practice.

ESTIMATES FOR MATERIAL AND EQUIPMENT COSTS

Responsibility for estimating the costs of materials and equipment usually lies in two areas. The engineers or designers must specify what materials and equipment will have to be bought and the purchasing department will be expected to find out how much these will cost and how long they will take to obtain.

If the purchasing organization is not allowed to partake in preparing the detailed estimates, a danger exists that when the time eventually comes to order the goods these will be obtained from the wrong suppliers at the wrong prices. It is far better if the big items of expense can be priced by getting quotations from the suppliers as early as possible. The buyer can keep all such quotations in readiness for the time when the project becomes live. If the purchasing department is to be held down to a materials budget, then it is only reasonable that its buyers should play the leading role in obtaining the cost estimates for materials and equipment.

Expenditure on materials and bought-out services can exceed half the total cost of a project. The proportion can be as high as 80 per cent. Unfortunately the purchasing function is not always given the recognition that it deserves in project management.

Materials need two types of estimate. These are:

1. The total expected cost, including all delivery and other charges.
2. The lead time, which is the elapsed time between placing the purchase order and receiving the goods at the point of use.

It might also be necessary to make estimates of other factors for operational purposes. For example the volume or weight of materials might be needed in order to arrange for storage, handling or onward transport.

If no detailed design has been carried out, no parts lists, bills of materials or other schedules will exist. In that case the engineers should be asked to prepare a provisional list of materials for each task. This may be impossible to carry out in exact detail, but the problem is not as difficult as it would first seem. In most project work the engineers have a good idea of the more significant and most expensive items that will have to be purchased. There might be special components, instruments, control gear, bearings, heavy weldments, castings, all depending of course on the type of project. In construction projects outline assumptions can be made for the types and quantities of bulk materials needed.

Foreknowledge of the main items of expense reduces the unknown area and improves the estimating accuracy. If all the important items can be listed and priced, the remaining miscellaneous purchases can be estimated by intelligent guesswork. If, for example, the known main components are going to account for 50 per cent of the total material costs, an error of 10 per cent in estimating the cost of the other materials would amount to only 5 per cent of the total.

Any estimate for materials is not complete unless all the costs of packing, transport, insurance, port duties, taxes and handling have been taken into account. The intending purchaser must be clear on what the price includes, and allowances must be made to take care of any services that are needed but not included in the quoted price.

Another cautionary word concerns the period of validity for quotations received from potential suppliers. Project cost estimates are often made many months – even years – before a contract is eventually awarded. Suppliers' quotations are typically valid for only 90 days or even less, so that there could be a problem with the materials cost budget or the availability of goods when the time eventually arrives for the purchase orders to be placed.

The general purpose estimating format shown in Figure 3.2 allows space for simple materials estimating requirements, like those needed for a small manufacturing project. For larger projects, especially those involving international movements, a format such as that shown in Figure 3.3 would be more appropriate.

COST ESTIMATE FOR MATERIALS AND BOUGHT EQUIPMENT		Project number or sales reference:										Estimate number: Case: Date:	
WBS No:				Compiled by:								Page of	
Cost code	Description	Specn. No (if known)	Proposed supplier	Unit	Unit cost F.O.B.	Quoted currency	Exchange rate used	Converted FOB cost	Qty	Project FOB cost	Ship mode	Freight cost	Taxes/ duties	Delivered cost
							Total delivered materials and equipment costs this page							

3.3 Cost estimating form for purchased materials and bought equipment on a capital project

BELOW THE LINE COSTS

When all the basic costs have been estimated, and the overheads have been added, a line can be drawn under them and the total should amount to the estimated net cost of sales. However, there are usually other costs which have to be evaluated and entered below that line.

Contingency Allowances

Additional costs are bound to arise as the result of design errors, production mistakes, material or component failures and the like. The degree to which these contingencies are going to add to the project costs will depend on many factors, including the type of project, the general competency of the firm, the soundness (or otherwise) of the engineering concepts and so on. Performance on previous projects should be a reliable pointer that can be used to decide just how much to allow on each new project to cover unforeseen circumstances. For a straightforward project, not entailing an inordinate degree of risk, an allowance set at 5 per cent of the above the line costs might be adequate.

The scope for adding an adequate contingency allowance will be restricted if there is high price competition from the market. If the perceived risk suggests the need for a high contingency allowance, the company might need to reconsider whether or not to undertake the project.

Cost Escalation

Every year wages and salaries increase, raw materials and bought-out components can cost more, transport becomes more expensive and plant and buildings absorb more money. All these increases correspond to the familiar decrease in the real value of money which is termed 'inflation'. This decay appears to be inevitable, and the rate is usually fairly predictable in the short term. In a country where the rate of inflation is 10 per cent, a project that was accurately estimated in 2015 to cost $5m (say) might cost an extra million dollars if its start were to be delayed for two years.

Unfortunately, cost inflation rates are not easy to predict over the long term, because they are subject to political, environmental and economic factors. However, a cost escalation allowance based on the best possible prediction should be made for any project whose duration is expected to exceed two years.

The rate chosen by the estimator for below the line cost escalation allowances might have to be negotiated and agreed with the customer (for example in defence or other contracts to be carried out for a national government).

The conditions of contract may allow the contractor to claim a price increase in the event of specified cost escalation events that are beyond its control (the usual case being a national industry wage award), but that is a different case from including escalation in quoted rates and prices as a below the line allowance.

Provisional Sums

It often happens, particularly in construction contracts, that the contractor foresees the possibility of additional work that might arise if particular difficulties are encountered when work actually starts. For example, a client may specify that materials are to be salvaged from a building during demolition work, to be re-used in the new construction. The contractor might wish to reserve its position by including a provisional sum, to be added to the project price in the event that the salvaged materials prove unsuitable for re-use. It is not unusual for a project quotation to include more than one provisional sum, covering several quite different eventualities.

Foreign Currencies

Most large projects involve transactions in currencies other than their own national currency. This can give rise to uncertainty and risk when the exchange rates vary. Some mitigation of this effect can be achieved if the contract includes safeguards, or if all quotations can be made and obtained in the home currency.

Common practice in project cost estimating is to nominate one currency as the control currency for the project, and then to convert all estimated costs into that currency using carefully chosen exchange rates. Although contractors would normally choose their home currency, projects may have to be quoted in foreign currencies if the terms of tendering so demand, and if the potential client insists.

Whether or not the contractor wishes to disclose the exchange rates used in reaching the final cost estimates, the rates used for all conversions must be shown clearly on the internally circulated estimating forms.

REVIEWING THE COST ESTIMATES

When the detailed estimates have been collected it should be possible to add them all up and declare a forecast of the whole project cost. However, it is never a bad plan to stand well back and view this picture from a different perspective. In particular, try converting the figures for labour times into man-years. Suppose that the engineering design work needed for a project appears to need 8750 man-hours. Taking 1750 man-hours or 50 man-weeks as being roughly equivalent to a man-year, division of the estimate shows that five man-years must be spent in order to complete the project design. Now assume that all the design is scheduled to be finished in the first six months of the programme. This could be viewed (simplistically) as a requirement of ten design engineers for six months.

The manager starting this project might receive a rude awakening on referring to records of past projects. These might well show that a project of similar size and complexity took not ten engineers for six months, but expenditure equivalent to ten engineers for a whole year. An apparent error of five man-years exists somewhere. This is, in any language, a king-sized problem. Part of its cause could be the failure of estimators to allow for that part of engineering design which is sometimes called 'after-issue', which means making corrections, incorporating unfunded modifications, answering engineering queries from the workforce or the customer, writing reports and putting records into archives.

It goes without saying that cost estimates for a project are extremely important. Any serious error could prove disastrous for the contractor – and for the customer too if it leads the contractor into financial difficulties. Every estimate should be checked as far as possible by a competent person who is independent of the original estimate compiler. Comparisons with actual cost totals for past projects (for all materials and labour – not just for the engineering design example given above) are valuable in checking that the new project cost estimate at least appears to be in the right ballpark.

4 *Managing Risk*

Everything we do, from getting out of bed in the morning to returning there at night, carries risk. It is not surprising that projects, which metaphorically (and sometimes literally) break new ground, attract many risks. Project risks can be predictable or completely unforeseeable. They might be caused by the physical elements or they could be political, economic, commercial, technical, or operational in origin. Freak events have been known to disrupt projects, such as the unexpected discovery of important archaeological remains or the decision by a few members of a rare protected species to establish their family home on what should have been the site of a new project.

Project risk management (and much of mainstream project management) is concerned with attempting to identify all the foreseeable risks, assessing the chance and severity of those risks, and then deciding what might be done to reduce their possible impact on the project or avoid them altogether.

Risks can occur at any stage in a project. Some are associated with particular tasks and others originate from outside the project and can manifest themselves without warning. Generally speaking, a risk event that occurs late in a project can be more costly in terms of time and money than a similar event nearer the start of the project. That is because as time passes there will be a greater value of work in progress and thus higher sunk costs at risk of loss or damage.

Some projects that are very small or which are similar to projects undertaken by the contractor in the past might not need special attention to risk management (other than obtaining some insurance cover). However, for any significant new project a risk management strategy must be developed, first to identify as many potential risks as possible and then to decide how to deal with them.

IDENTIFYING THE POSSIBLE RISKS

Risks can occur in any kind of project and they can range from the obvious to the most unexpected and bizarre. In a lifetime spent with projects I have known risk events ranging in scale from a tragic underground mining disaster to an exploding hearing aid battery (which blew the unfortunate lady's hat off). Risk events can even happen after the project is finished and handed over. Business change and IT projects seem to be particularly prone to risk of failure, with huge losses of money. With this vast breeding ground for possible risks it is apparent that the risk manager's first problem is to identify the risks that might affect the project.

Checklists (which should grow in size and value as companies gain more project experience) are a good starting point for listing the foreseeable risks. Studying the history of similar projects can also highlight possible problems and help the project manager to learn from the mistakes, accidents and experiences of others.

A brainstorming meeting of key staff is a good method for identifying all the possible risks (along with many of the improbable ones). Much depends on how the brainstorming session is conducted. The meeting leader should encourage an atmosphere of 'anything goes', so that participants feel free to propose even the most bizarre risk possibilities without fear of ridicule. All suggestions, without exception, should be recorded for subsequent appraisal and analysis.

RISK APPRAISAL AND ANALYSIS

Once identified and listed, risks can be ranked according to the probability of their occurrence and the severity of the impact if they should occur. This process allows the most improbable risks listed during brainstorming to be removed, but it should highlight those risks that are most likely to happen or which would have the greatest potential impact on the project. For this analysis the possible causes and effects of every identified risk have to be considered.

Qualitative Risk Assessment

Qualitative risk analysis involves considering each risk in a purely descriptive way. We have to imagine various characteristics of the risk and the physical effect that it could have on the project.

Fault-tree analysis and Ishikawa fishbone diagrams (not described here) are methods used by reliability and safety engineers to consider and analyse the effects of faults in design and construction, but they can be adapted easily for project management.

A common project management method, which also has its roots in reliability engineering, is failure, mode and effect analysis (FMEA). Failure mode and effect analysis starts by considering possible risk events (failure modes) and then proceeds to predict their possible effects. Figure 4.1 shows part of a simple FMEA chart. This illustration contains only three items, but there might be hundreds in a large project. This is a qualitative process because there is no attempt to give each risk a priority ranking number or to quantify the damage if the risk should occur.

	Item	Failure mode	Cause of failure	Effect	Recommended action
1	Project manager's car	Engine refuses to start	Poor maintenance	Project manager marooned at remote site with no other means of transport	Improve vehicle maintenance procedures. Consider replacing the car.
2	Main building	Building collapses during installation of heavy machinery	Errors in floor loading calculations	Personal injuries Project delays Loss of reputation	Triple check key structural calculations
3			Floor slabs incorrectly poured	Personal injuries Project delays Loss of reputation	Ensure operatives get good training and instruction. Employ competent site engineering manager.

4.1   Part of a failure, mode and effect analysis (FMEA)

Quantitative Risk Analysis

Quantitative risk analysis goes at least one stage further than qualitative analysis by attempting to quantify the outcome of a risk event or to attach a numerical score (rank) to the risk according to its perceived priority for arranging preventive or mitigating action.

Although all quantitative methods produce 'actual' numbers they can give a false sense of precision. The results are based on only on estimates and human judgement. Those judgements might be fundamentally flawed, mistaken or simply too difficult for any person to make with any degree of certainty.

Failure mode effect and criticality analysis (FMECA) is a common method for attempting to quantify and rank risks. The example in Figure 4.2 is based on the FMEA illustrated in Figure 4.1 but now contains ranking assessments. The numbers written against each risk in the columns headed 'Chance', 'Severity' and 'Detection difficulty' are allocated on a scale of 1 to 5, where 5 is at the highest end of the perceived impact scale. Multiplying these three numbers for each particular risk gives that risk a ranking number. The higher this ranking number, the greater must be the management attention given to prevent the risk from occurring or to mitigate its effects should it happen.

Item 2 in Figure 4.2, for example, considers the possibility and potential seriousness of a building collapse. This is for a building created as part of a project, and the collapse in question might happen during the installation of heavy machinery on an upper-level floor. If the floor has been incorrectly designed or constructed, it might not be sufficiently strong to carry the weight of the machinery. The assessor clearly thinks this is unlikely to happen because they have ranked chance at the

Item	Failure mode	Cause of failure	Effect	Chance	Severity	Detection difficulty	Rank
1 Project manager's car	Engine refuses to start	Poor maintenance	Project manager marooned at remote site with no other means of transport	2	1	3	6
2 Main building	Building collapses during installation of heavy machinery	Errors in floor loading calculations	Personal injuries. Project delays. Loss of reputation.	1	5	3	15
3	Building collapses during installation of heavy machinery	Floor slabs incorrectly poured	Personal injuries. Project delays. Loss of reputation.	1	5	2	10

4.2   Failure, mode, effect and criticality analysis (FMECA)

bottom end of the 1–5 scale. There is no doubt, however, that if this event did occur it would be extremely serious, so the severity has been marked as 5.

Detection difficulty means the difficulty of noticing the cause of a risk in time to prevent the risk event. In this example of possible floor collapse, the risk assessor thinks that although the chance of a design error is very low, the difficulty of spotting a mistake if it did occur would be fairly high (3 on the scale of 1–5).

The product of these three parameters, $1 \times 5 \times 3$ gives a total ranking number of 15. Theoretically, when this exercise has been performed on every item in the list, the list can be sorted in descending sequence of these ranking numbers, so that risks with the highest priority for management attention come at the top of the list.

Some assessors use weighted parameters. For example, it might be considered that the severity of the risk should play a higher part in deciding ranking priority, so the severity column could be marked on a higher scale, say from 1–10. Item 2 in Figure 4.2 might then be marked 9 on this extended scale, which would increase the ranking factor for this item from 15 to 27.

RISK REGISTER

When all the known risks have been listed, assessed and ranked it is time to consider what might be done about them. That process requires that all potential risks be listed in a risk register (or risk log). An example of a risk register page is shown in Figure 4.3. This is modelled closely on the FMECA method demonstrated in Figure 4.2 but with the following noticeable additions:

- an ID number for each risk listed;
- space for noting any action required;
- a column headed 'Action by' in which the name of the person or manager responsible for taking action for each risk can be entered.

The risk register should be reviewed and updated regularly throughout the life of the project. It is advisable to use the computer to sort the risks according to their ranking, with the highest-ranked risks placed at the top.

Risk ID	Date registered	Risk description and consequences	Probability P = 1-3	Impact (severity) S = 1- 3	Detection difficulty D = 1-3	Risk ranking P x S x D	Recommended mitigating or risk avoidance action	Action by:

4.3   Example of a risk register (or risk log) format

METHODS FOR DEALING WITH RISKS

When all the known risks have been identified, assessed, ranked and registered it is time to consider what might be done about them. The resulting decisions must be entered in the two right-hand columns of the risk register.

The project manager usually has a range of options about how to deal with each possible risk:

1. *Avoid the risk* – the only way to avoid a risk is to remove all the possible causes, which could even mean deciding not to do the job at all.

2. *Take precautions to prevent or mitigate risk impact* – this is a most important part of risk management, needing the active participation of managers and relevant staff. It needs a high-level risk prevention strategy combined with executive determination to ensure that all preventive measures are always followed throughout all parts of the organization. It requires the creation of a risk prevention culture, covering all aspects of project tasks, health and safety and consideration for the environment. Here are a few examples of the many possible practical measures, chosen and listed at random:
   - high security fencing to reduce the chance of gatecrashers at an open air pop festival;
   - provision of marquees at a garden party in case of rain;
   - regular inspection and testing of electrical equipment and cables to ensure safe operation;
   - double-checking to detect errors in design calculations for vital project components or structures;
   - provision of back-up electrical power supplies for vital operations, essential services and computers;
   - frequent back-up and secure offline storage of data;
   - avoidance of trailing electric cables in pedestrian areas;
   - ensuring that means of escape routes in buildings are always clear of obstructions and that smoke screen doors are kept closed;
   - regular fire drills, testing of fire alarms and emergency lighting;
   - on-the-job training of back-up staff to understudy key roles in the organization;
   - regular inspection and maintenance of lifts and hoists;
   - provision of safety clothing and equipment to protect workers, and enforcement of their use;
   - restricted access to hazardous areas;
   - provision of secure handrails and good lighting to all stairways;
   - choosing the time of year most likely to provide fair weather for outdoor projects;
   - adequate training of all those operating potentially hazardous machinery;
   - regular financial audits and the installation of procedures to identify or deter fraud;
   - and so on, and so on: this list could be very long.
3. *Accept the risk* – rain might make the day chosen for office relocation miserable for all concerned but the risk would have to be accepted. There are numerous small things that can go wrong during the course of any project. Many of these risks can be accepted in the knowledge that their effect is not likely to be serious.
4. *Share the risk* – if a project, or a substantial part of it, appears to carry very high risk, the contractor might seek one or more partners to undertake the work as a joint venture. Then the impact of any failure would be shared among the partners. Sharing a risk big enough to ruin one company might reduce

its impact to little more than a temporary inconvenience when it is shared between two or more companies.

5. *Limit the risk* – there are occasions when project risks should only be accepted with safeguards to limit their potential effect. A good example is a task or project, perhaps for pure research, that cannot be clearly defined at the outset. The stage-gating procedure outlined at the beginning of Chapter 2 is usually suitable for this purpose. Some project closure tasks carry the risk that spending on them could go on for too long after the project has been delivered. One way to mitigate this is to allow only named individuals to spend time on closure tasks and to impose a strict time limit.

6. *Transfer the risk to a third party* – some risks, or substantial parts of them, can be transferred to another party. By far the most common method relies on obtaining insurance from an insurance broker or underwriter. Figure 4.4 summarizes some of the insurance obligations and options available to project managers.

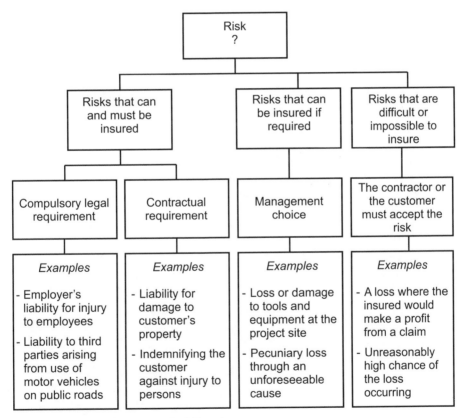

4.4 Insurance options and obligations

OBTAINING INSURANCE

Insurance can be sought directly from an underwriter, or through a broker; preferably one with a good reputation and experienced in the insured's type of project activity. The insurer will need to be supplied with sufficient information for the risk to be adequately defined, and the contractor will be expected to inform the insurer of any change of circumstances likely to affect the risks insured. The insurer may wish to make investigations or even follow up the project work using its own experts.

Professional advice from experienced insurers can often be of great benefit in reducing risks, especially in the areas of health and safety and crime prevention. The time to seek such advice is before work on the project starts.

5 *Organizing the Project*

An effective organization ensures that clear lines of authority exist, and that every member of the project knows what he or she must do to make the project a success. This is part of the management communication framework, essential for motivating all the staff employed. A well-motivated group can be a joy to work with. A badly informed group, with vague responsibilities and ambiguous levels of status and authority, is likely to be poorly motivated, slow to achieve results, costly to run and frustrating to manage.

Good management communications include adequate feedback paths through and across the organization. These allow progress to be monitored, difficulties to be reported back to executive management and expert specialist advice on technical or commercial problems to be sought and given.

Every company has its own ideas about how to organize itself and its work. It is highly probable that if three companies doing similar work could be compared, three different organization structures would be found. Further, all three companies might be successful, implying that it is not always possible to declare firmly that there is one best organization solution. This chapter cannot, therefore, dictate exactly how every project should be organized. Instead, it describes the advantages and disadvantage of possible organization options, so that readers can judge which might be appropriate for their project.

For many people these arguments are academic, because most project managers are appointed to an organization that already exists and have no authority to change it. Power to create organizational change is owned by more senior management, so perhaps it is they who should be reading this chapter.

MATRIX ORGANIZATIONS

Line and Function Organization

Many businesses are organized as a line and function matrix structure. Senior managers occupy the top positions, and specialists (such as operations managers, accountants and marketing managers) report to them. Other staff occupy the lower layers. The whole is like a family tree, following hierarchical management patterns that were laid down many centuries ago in the army and the church. This kind of organization usually works well for companies whose operations are continuous and routine.

Coordination Matrix Organizations

Planning and coordination difficulties arise when a line and function organization encounters its first project. Senior company managers are accustomed to looking down into a number of separate departments that perform routine functions. No person has the time and skills necessary to plan the project and follow it through all the stages of its life cycle.

This difficulty can be overcome to a great extent by appointing a project manager or coordinator. In a manufacturing company, the result might be the kind of organization charted in Figure 5.1. This arrangement is known as a coordination matrix (or coordinated matrix or functional matrix).

The project manager provides a focus for the new project but has no line authority. Here the project manager is a planner and coordinator and can only request that project tasks are carried out according to the schedule. Organizational theorists would call this a staff position in a line and staff organization. If functional managers ignore the project manager or argue among themselves, the project manager's remedy is to appeal to senior line management for help.

A coordination matrix has the big advantage that it is very easy to establish and calls for no change in the existing company organization. It is not disruptive. When the project is over, the company simply carries on as before (except that it must decide what will happen to the project manager who is now without a project).

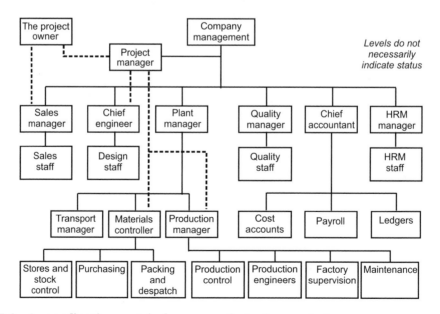

5.1 A coordination matrix for a manufacturing project

Matrix Solutions for Multiple Projects

When a company handles several projects simultaneously, it can appoint a project manager for each project and set up a matrix organization similar to that shown in Figure 5.2 (for a manufacturing company) or Figure 5.3 (for a company engaged in petrochemical, mining or other large capital projects).

The way in which power is apportioned between these project managers and the various departmental managers can vary considerably from one company to another. Organization charts cannot show all the subtle nuances of power. So Figures 5.2 and 5.3 do not show how power is distributed between the project managers and the functional managers. Thus these charts remain valid for the variations of the matrix that will now be described.

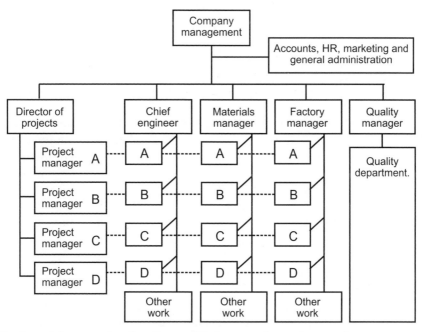

5.2   A matrix organization for multiple manufacturing projects

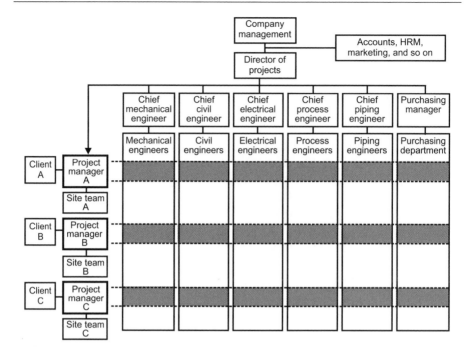

5.3   A matrix organization for mining and petrochemical projects

Weak Matrix

A weak matrix describes any form of matrix organization in which the project manager's power is low compared with managers of the specialist functions. Thus a coordination matrix is an example of a weak matrix.

Balanced Matrix

The balanced matrix (or overlay matrix) provides for a balance of power and authority between the project managers and the functional department managers. All managers are expected to work together harmoniously and make joint decisions (for example on the allocation of resources). This is a common form of matrix and is elegant in theory. However, it depends on universal goodwill and is not an ideal solution for every project case.

Stronger Forms of the Matrix

In a strong matrix the project manager's authority is greater than that of the functional managers, at least as far as work allocation and progressing is concerned. The intention is that the functional managers nominate members of their departments to work for the project managers on specified projects. The people assigned report principally to the project managers (although they might remain physically located in their home departments).

The very strongest matrix form is the secondment matrix, where functional managers must release their staff completely to work for project managers for as long as they are needed (which usually involves temporary physical relocation).

PROJECT TEAM ORGANIZATION

It is, of course, possible to arrange things differently from the matrix options described above. A complete work group or team can be created for each project as a self-contained unit with the project manager placed at its head. The project manager is given direct line authority over the team.

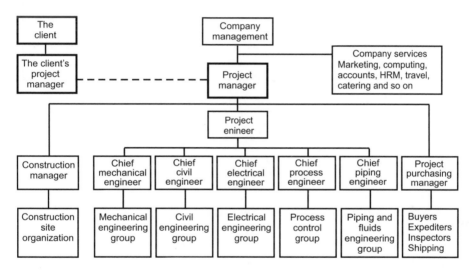

5.4 A project team organization

The example shown in Figure 5.4 is a project team organization that might be set up for a petrochemical or mining project. The project manager is in direct command, with complete authority over the team members.

Communications across the various technical and professional disciplines are easier and faster in a team when compared to a matrix. All members of the team identify with the project and can (at least in the short term) be strongly motivated towards achieving the project goals.

The key members of the team should preferably be located near each other, in the same building if possible. Ideally, an office should be provided for use as a 'project war room', where team members can meet formally or informally whenever they wish. Drawings, charts and plans can be displayed on the war room tables and walls.

Project Task Forces

A task force is an extreme form of a project team. It demands total dedication to the project, sometimes almost with fanaticism. A task force can generate the highest levels of motivation and appreciation of urgency. It is the ideal arrangement for rescuing a project that is in danger of running late or failing altogether.

The task force leader must possess determination and drive in abundance. He/She should also be experienced in the project management arts: if not, it might be prudent to engage an external consultant, either to lead the task force or to provide urgent on-the-job training and guidance. A manager brought in specifically to rescue a failing project is sometimes known colloquially as a hero project manager.

Task force members will work even more effectively if they can be located together, away from their normal workplaces, and near their project war room.

Task forces in manufacturing projects

A self-contained project team might seem to be impracticable in a manufacturing company owing to the capital invested in the general manufacturing facilities. Expensive plant cannot usually be allocated for task force use and set aside full-time for the project, no matter how urgent the work is. This problem can be solved by including in the task force managers (or their senior delegates) from all the departments involved in executing the project. When the project demands the urgent use of scarce or expensive common resources, the relevant task force member will have the authority to instruct his or her home department to carry out the work with maximum priority.

Task forces in management change projects

Most management change projects begin with studies that have to be kept confidential, to avoid creating unfounded but damaging rumours. This is especially important where the project might lead to company reorganization or relocation and redundancies. For example, I remember a company relocation project where various locations throughout southern England and the Midlands were considered. News of management visits to these places leaked out, causing much unnecessary unrest among the staff. In the event there was no move, but much damage had been done to depress morale throughout the company. The time for openness and consultation with staff must come, but not until the results of a completed study have suggested a preferred solution.

A task force comprising senior delegates from all company departments that would be affected by the management change project can be set to work in a secure office, allowing the study work to be carried out in secrecy. When external consultants are engaged to lead the study, the presence on the task force of people who know their departments' operations intimately can prevent expensive and damaging errors and omissions in the proposed solutions.

TEAM OR MATRIX: WHICH ORGANIZATION IS BEST?

Team Pros and Cons

Project teams have the advantage that they can each be directed to the successful completion of one project. A team can be completely autonomous. It is provided with and relies on its own staff and facilities. There is no clash of priorities resulting from a clamour of different project managers in competition for scarce, shared resources.

An important aspect of motivation is the generation of a team spirit, in which all members of the team strive to meet common goals. It is clearly easier to establish a team spirit when a project team actually exists (as opposed to the case where the people are dispersed over a matrix organization that has to deal with many projects).

If the work is being conducted for a national defence contract, or for any other project that requires a secret or confidential environment, the establishment of a project team greatly helps the organizers to contain all the work and its information within secure boundaries.

However, unless the project is very large, the individual specialist subgroups within the team will be too small to allow optimum flexibility of labour and other resources. For example, where a common manufacturing facility of 100 people is coping with several projects, the absence of a few workers through sickness might result in some rescheduling but would be unlikely to cause disaster. If, on the other hand, a project team had been set up to include its own independent manufacturing group, perhaps justifying the employment of only six people, the infection of three of these with influenza could set the project back by weeks.

There is a danger that professional people working alone in small project teams are deprived of the benefits of working in a department with colleagues of their own specialist discipline. It is less easy for them to discuss technical problems with their peers or have access to the valuable fund of technical and professional data (historic and current) that such specialist functional groups accumulate.

Even if a project is of sufficient size to justify its own exclusive team, not all the problems of project coordination will necessarily be overcome. Very often it might be found impossible to house all the participants under one roof, or even in the same locality. Although team organization might be logical and ideal for the project, a general lack of coordination between the functions is still a possible risk.

A big problem with a project team organization is realized when the project end is in sight. Team members will have concerns about their future work, or indeed whether or not there will be any future work for them at all. That concern is a powerful demotivator and can lead to a slowing down of work in an attempt to delay project completion and put off the evil day.

Another possible danger with a team is that something could go seriously wrong with the project after its supposed completion, with expert attention required from the team's engineers to satisfy the customer and put matters right. If the team no longer exists, and the engineers who designed the project have been dispersed, events could take an embarrassing, even ugly, turn.

Matrix Pros and Cons

The matrix option allows the establishment of specialist functional groups which have 'eternal life', independent of the duration of individual projects. This continuity of work promotes the gradual build-up of expertise and experience. Specialist skills are concentrated. Pooling of skills provides for flexibility in deploying resources.

Each member of every specialist group enjoys a reasonably stable basis for employment (provided the order book is full). There is a clear promotion path within the discipline up to at least chief engineer level, and each person in the group is able to compete against his or her colleagues for more senior positions within the group as vacancies arise in the long term.

Performance assessment of each individual, and any recommendation for promotion, improved salary or other benefits, is carried out by a chief engineer or other manager of the same professional discipline within the stable group. This is more likely to result in a fair assessment and employee satisfaction. These possibilities are not readily available to the specialist professional person working alone in a multidisciplined project team.

The matrix organization has its own characteristic disadvantages. Not least of these is the split responsibility that each group member faces between their functional line manager and the project manager in a balanced matrix. Employees are expected to serve two masters at the same time. That violates the long-established principle of unity of command. Personal stress and conflict will arise if an individual receives conflicting instructions from the project manager and his or her functional manager.

Summary

So, team or matrix? The arguments will no doubt continue as to which is the better of the two organizations. Some of the pros and cons are summarized in Figure 5.5. As a general guide, large projects of long duration will probably benefit from the formation of dedicated project teams. Matrix organizations are indicated for companies which handle a number of small projects in which neither the amount of resources nor the timescale needed for each project is great.

On a more personal note, think of yourself for a moment as being a member of the project organization, and imagine how each of the different possible organizations would affect your motivation and job satisfaction. If you have the power to choose the organization structure, that imaginative experience might lead you to make the correct choice.

Characteristic	Organization indicated	
	Team	Matrix
Maximum authority for the project manager	●	
Freedom from duplicated or ambiguous lines of command	●	
Maximum motivation of staff to meet difficult targets	●	
High security of information: by enclosing work in secure areas	●	
High security of information: by restricting the number of staff who need to know about the work	●	
Most flexible deployment of resources		●
Most effective use across the company of those with rare specialist skills or knowledge		●
Large project, employing many people for a long duration	●	
Several small simultaneous projects, each needing a few people for a short time		●
Career motivation of individuals: opportunities for promotion within a person's specialist discipline		●
Career motivation of individuals: through long-term continuity and relative stability of the organization		●
Post-design support to construction or commissioning staff		●
Efficient post-project services to the customer		●
Establishment of 'retained engineering' information files and databanks from which future projects can benefit		●

5.5   Project team versus a balance matrix

HYBRID ORGANIZATIONS

Sometimes companies adopt a hybrid organization, operating a matrix organization in general, but with teams set up for certain projects when the need arises.

An example of such a hybrid organization is shown in Figure 5.6. This one is arranged principally as a matrix. However, if a project should arise which requires predominantly one specialist function, the company can appoint a project manager from within the relevant specialist group, who then manages a project team that is contained within the group.

For example, a project to install a new electrical generator in an existing plant might be a project that could be handled entirely by a team within the electrical department. Similarly, a land reclamation project could be assigned solely to the

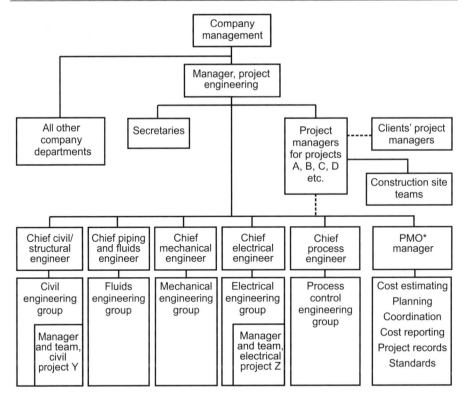

* PMO = project management office

5.6 A hybrid organization

civil engineering group, who would set up their own internal team to deal with it under a civil engineer as project manager.

CONTRACT MATRIX ORGANIZATIONS

A contract matrix is often used in construction projects. An example is shown in Figure 5.7. Here the project owner (the customer or client) has engaged a managing contractor to design the project, carry out purchasing, hire subcontractors and generally manage all the activities at a construction site.

The organization chart shows that many of the companies involved in the project will have their own project managers, in addition to the principal project manager employed by the main contractor.

The project in this example is being funded by a bank, which has lent funds on condition that the project owner finds a guarantor who is willing to underwrite a substantial part of the lending risk. In the UK, for example, the Export Credits

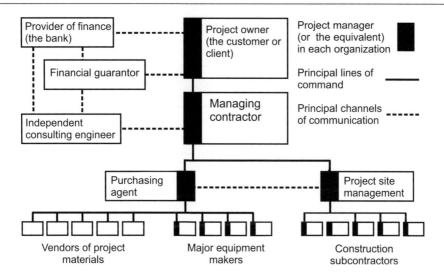

5.7 A contract matrix organization

Guarantee Department (ECGD) acts as guarantor for some projects carried out for overseas clients.

Both the bank and the guarantor need expert independent advice, because they are usually financial experts with little knowledge of the design and completion of construction projects. This expert advice has been provided in the example of Figure 5.7 by a professional engineering organization. This organization, sometime known simply as 'the engineer', can inspect progress and certify all significant claims for payments so that monies are only paid against work that has actually been performed correctly and in the quantities listed on the contractor's invoices.

JOINT VENTURE PROJECTS

For very large projects two or more companies might agree to combine their resources and share the technical problems, expense and risk by forming a consortium or joint venture company. This approach will add yet another complication to the organization. An outline example of a joint venture organization is given in Figure 5.8.

For any complex project, apart from the obvious need to define responsibilities and all the contractual details, it is vital that the lines of communication between all the parties are clearly established and specified. It is not unusual to find projects where the participants are separated by international borders and thousands of miles. The volume of information for a large project, whether in the form of drawings, other technical documents, commercial correspondence, queries, and even hotel and travel arrangements can be mind-boggling.

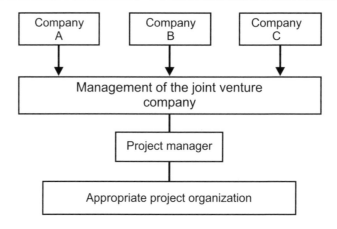

5.8   One form of joint venture organization for a large project

THE PROJECT MANAGER

If the objectives of project management could be condensed into responsibility for ensuring work completion within time and cost restrictions, these goals could be achieved by a variety of approaches. One project manager might operate successfully by inducing fear and trepidation in subordinates, so that his every word is seen as a command to be instantly obeyed. Another person might achieve the same results through gentle but firm persuasion. The essential element here is the ability to motivate people, by whatever means: the seasoned expert will be able to vary his or her management style according to the response of the individual being managed.

The average project participant will appreciate being led by a project manager who displays competence, makes clear decisions, gives precise achievable instructions, delegates well, listens to and accepts sound advice, is enthusiastic and confident, and thus generally commands respect by example and qualities of leadership.

The Project Manager as a Hunter-gatherer of Information

Most project managers are given information that is incomplete, unduly optimistic, inaccurate or deliberately misleading. Project managers will learn to check much of the information that they receive, particularly by knowing what questions to ask to probe its validity. As they gain experience of a particular organization they should become capable of assessing the reliability of individuals or departments, so that they can apply 'confidence factors' to the data which those individuals or departments submit and the stories that they tell.

Project managers must be able to extract the salient facts from a set of data or a particular set of circumstances. They must then be able to use these facts to best effect by taking action themselves or, where that is not possible, by reporting significant problems to executive management (with unimportant and irrelevant material filtered out).

All project managers know the frustration caused not simply by receiving inaccurate information, but by receiving no information at all. Data deficiencies can take the form of delayed instructions (or approvals) from the customer, late information from subcontractors and vendors, and tardy release of design and other information within the project manager's own company. It can be difficult to obtain reliable and regular reports of cost and progress from far-flung project outposts, particularly where the individuals responsible feel themselves to be remote and outside the project manager's immediate authority or are educated to standards below those of the more fully developed nations.

The ability to gather and assess relevant data is, therefore, an essential property for project management. It is no good expecting to obtain the complete picture and manage a project simply by sitting fixed behind a desk for the duration of the project. Project managers must take (and be seen to take) an active interest. They should visit personally and regularly those parts of the organization on which the project is dependent (a process sometimes known as 'management by walking about'). It might be necessary for the project manager to visit vendors, subcontractors, the customer and a remote construction site at suitable intervals in order to gather facts, resolve local disputes, generate enthusiasm, or simply to witness progress at first hand.

General Knowledge and Current Awareness

Project managers in the age of technology could be described as specialists. Their background may be in one of the specialist engineering or other professional disciplines and they will certainly need to be trained in one or more of the current special project management techniques if they are to operate effectively. Nevertheless the term 'specialist' can be misleading, since much of the project manager's time will be taken up with coordinating the activities of project participants from a wide variety of administrative, professional, technical and craft backgrounds. This work, far from requiring specialization, demands a sufficient general understanding of the work carried out by those participants for the project manager to be able to discuss the work sensibly, understand all the commercial and technical data received, and appreciate (or question) any reported problems.

The project manager should understand the administrative procedures used throughout the project organization. If a person is asked to handle a flow of project data between different departments, he or she should be able to use their understanding of the administration and its procedures to arrange for the information to be presented in the form most likely to be helpful to the various recipients.

There is little doubt that project management tools, techniques and philosophy will continue to change. Most project managers need to keep abreast of development, undergoing training or retraining whenever necessary, and passing this training on to other members of the organization where appropriate.

Some new developments will advance the practice of project management in general and others will not. Some practices and techniques will be more useful to a particular project situation than others. The project manager must be able to choose, use or adapt the most appropriate management methods for the particular project. Temptation to impose unsuitable methods on an organization for the sole reason that they represent the height of current fashion must be resisted.

Support, Cooperation and Training for the Project Manager

No matter how experienced, competent, enthusiastic and intelligent the person chosen for the job of project manager, he or she cannot expect to operate effectively alone, without adequate support and cooperation. This obviously includes the willing cooperation of all staff engaged on the project, whether they report to the project manager in the line organization or not. But it also includes support from higher management in the organization, who must at least ensure the provision of essential finance, accommodation, facilities, equipment, manpower and other resources when they are needed, and the availability of suitable staff.

Just as those working on the project need to be well motivated, so does the project manager. Supportive higher management who show constructive and helpful interest in the project can go a long way to achieve this. They can also help in the longer term by providing opportunities for training as new techniques or management systems are developed.

A person who is responsible for the allocation and progressing of project tasks will inevitably be called upon to decide priorities or criticize progress. Project Managers must often arrange for the issue of work instructions knowing that they have no direct authority over all the departments involved. In a matrix organization particularly, departmental managers alone are responsible for the performance, day-to-day management and work allocation within their own departments. I have even known cases where departmental managers have told project managers to keep out of their departments. In such circumstances the project manager's influence can only be exerted as reflected authority from higher management, without whose full backing the project manager will be ineffective.

The main show of authority which the project manager can wield stems from his or her personality and the ability to lead and motivate others. Nowadays, discipline seldom implies the imposition of rigid authoritarian regimes or management by fear through the constant threat of dismissal or other punitive action. Mutual cooperation and established job satisfaction are the more likely elements of an effective approach. I know from personal experience how respect and even comradeship from juniors can make a project manager's job rewarding and relatively trouble-free.

There will, of course, be occasions when firm discipline has to be exercised. Then, in the last resort, the full backing and support of higher management must be available as a reserve force which the project manager can call upon in any hour of need.

The project manager should keep abreast of new developments in project management. Various training establishments arrange project management seminars where, in addition to the formal training given, delegates from different companies are able to meet and discuss mutual problems and solutions, and exchange views and experiences generally. The effectiveness of these individuals and of the profession as a whole must benefit from this type of exchange.

Just as important as the project manager's own training is the creation of an enlightened and informed attitude to modern project management methods among all those in the project organization. Ideally, when the objectives of a particular project are outlined the project manager should ensure that participating managers, engineers and line supervisors have at least been given an elementary grounding in the appreciation of scheduling, principles of cost and progress control, and the interpretation of associated computer reports. This should all be with specific relevance to the procedures chosen for use on the actual project.

Training or instructions should be given in the use of the various documents to be used and (where appropriate) in the active use of relevant computer applications. There is a danger that people who are suddenly asked to work with unfamiliar techniques and procedures, without sufficient training or explanation, will fail to cooperate. If participating staff understand the procedures and the reasons for them, their cooperation is far more likely to be forthcoming and effective.

PROJECT MANAGEMENT OFFICE (PMO)

Unless the organization is too small to support the additional expense, it makes sense to set up a central project management support or project services group, usually called a project management office. This is staffed with people (not too many!) who are capable of the day-to-day chores of planning; resource scheduling, cost estimating, work progressing, cost and progress reporting and general supervision of the company's project management computer applications.

A PMO can be used in most kinds of project organization. It can exist within a pure project team, where it will serve and report directly to the project manager. If the organization is a multi-project matrix or a hybrid organization, the PMO can be regarded almost as one of the departmental functions (an arrangement illustrated Figure 5.6).

A PMO concentrates a company's expertise in the techniques of project management, just as any functional grouping can enhance a particular professional discipline. Centralization helps to standardize project administration procedures across all projects in a company. A PMO is the logical place from which to coordinate all parts of the project cycle, from authorization to closedown. It can also administer procedures such as project registration and change control.

Some powerful project management computer systems, especially those handling multi-project scheduling, are best placed under the supervision of specially trained planners and schedulers and the most appropriate place for them is within a PMO.

6 *Work Breakdown Structures*

This chapter describes the work breakdown process (WBS), which means breaking the project down into manageable chunks from which work can be allocated to departmental managers and other members of the project organization.

THE WBS CONCEPT

A work breakdown structure is a logical, hierarchical tree of all the tasks needed to complete a project. The top of the tree is the project itself. The next layer or level down contains the main *work packages*. Levels below that progressively get more detailed until the bottom level is reached: this shows all the smallest day-to-day tasks or project components. Anyone familiar with the arrangement of folders and files in a computer memory, or who has researched their ancestral family tree, should be familiar with this idea. The work breakdown concept is also seen in the 'goes-into' charts that engineers and designers use when organizing their drawings, bills of materials and parts lists into a logical pattern.

   The first example of a WBS in this chapter is for an imaginary project to design and develop a prototype automobile. Figure 6.1 is a summarized version of the top WBS levels. All engineers will recognize how this WBS corresponds closely to a goes-into chart. It shows how the major components of the vehicle relate to each other. One can also see how this breakdown might suggest the allocation of design managers or engineers to different parts of a project.

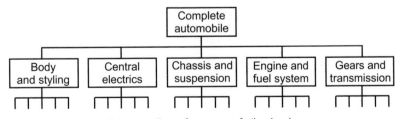

The work breakdown continues for as many further levels as necessary

6.1   Simplified WBS for an automobile project

Logical Interfacing and Completeness

In addition to regarding the work breakdown as a family tree, it is also possible to visualize it as a jigsaw puzzle with every piece in its right place and with no piece missing to spoil the total picture. This is sometimes difficult to achieve, but risks of omission can be reduced by the use of suitable checklists. A brainstorming meeting can help to identify all the tasks for a new project with no comparable predecessor.

A method must be found that identifies each piece of the puzzle and denotes its position in relation to all the other pieces. That's rather like giving each piece map coordinates or an address. This can be achieved by devising a logical coding system (coding systems are outlined later in this chapter).

WBS Examples

A few people find difficulty in constructing work breakdown charts and I have seen students' coursework in which work breakdown charts have been confused with organization charts. Thus this chapter contains a sprinkling of WBS examples taken from various kinds of projects.

Project for a national charity fundraising week

Much of the work carried out by any charity must be devoted to collecting as much money as possible. Without such mercenary efforts a charity would not be able to render its humanitarian service. Thus the Society for Impoverished Writers has decided to organize an annual national fundraising week. Being sensible people, the charity managers have decided to treat this as a project, and one of the first things that they must do is to draw a WBS. The result could be like that shown in Figure 6.2.

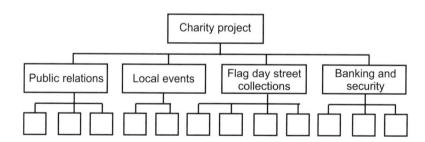

6.2 WBS for a national charity fundraising week

This WBS has four main elements or principal work packages, and one can easily imagine that a different senior manager would be made responsible for each of these.

One manager will organize all public relations activities nationwide that tell the public about this special week. Thus the second level WBS breakdown for this public relations work package might include newspaper advertising, television commercials, posters, billboards, mailshots and so on.

Someone else can be put in charge of 'local events'. These will be arranged through a network of volunteers, and might include coffee mornings, students' rags, village fetes, sponsored walks and so forth.

No fundraising week would be complete without its flag day, in which volunteers make their presence felt in the streets of towns and cities throughout the land, carrying tin cans with slots in their tops for the receipt of donations. Optimists might even be seen carrying buckets for this work. Someone must organize the production of cans and their labels, find the volunteers, and make sure that all the cans are eventually returned to headquarters.

In all events where large sums of money are concerned there is scope for fraud and theft. So the Society for Impoverished Writers has included a task for overseeing the handling of all the money collected, to ensure that it ends up in the charity's bank and not in the pockets of thieves.

A copper mining project

One of the world's largest mining organizations has discovered deposits of copper ore in the middle of a large uninhabited area of scrubland and desert. The region is utterly devoid of any sign of civilization (this has similarities from projects in my past experience). Figure 6.3 shows a small part of the large work breakdown structure that would be needed.

Each of the main work packages at level one is concerned with a significant part of the whole mining community, complete with a brand new township containing facilities for the mine's construction and operating staff, their families and visitors. There is nothing at the site when this project begins except a camp and lots of hope. Thus everything has to be provided from scratch for this enormous project, including all the infrastructure of the new township.

Level two of this WBS expands each of the work packages from level one. Only one of these is shown in Figure 6.3, which is for the mining complex itself. This mining complex includes all the buildings and plant necessary for extracting the ore from deep underground and then processing it to produce bars of almost pure copper.

One part of the mining complex is the concentrator plant, which crushes the rock to a powder and removes much of the non-copper-bearing material. This has its own place in level three of the WBS.

This work breakdown structure must be continued until, eventually, the lowest levels are reached in which all the tiniest components of the new mine town and plant are listed. Thus this WBS can be drawn only at the upper levels when the project starts. The very lowest levels will not be known until much of the design has been completed.

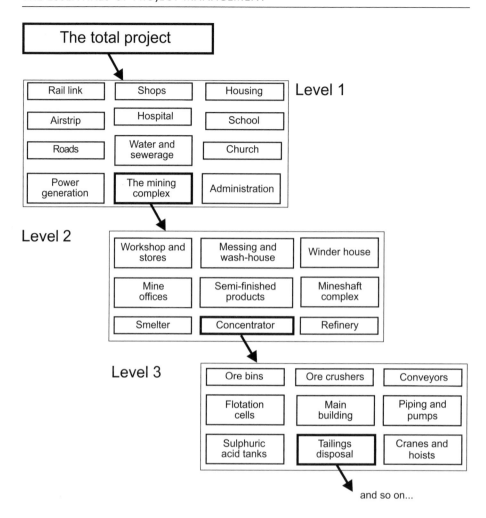

6.3   Part of the upper WBS levels for a copper mine

A large wedding project

This is an example of a *management project*. When the project is finished there is no tangible result and nothing visible to 'hand over' to a project owner – except perhaps a marriage certificate, a photograph album and a slice or two of wedding cake. When judged against the scale of many modern projects, organizing a wedding might seem to be a trivial affair. However, suppose that *you* have been asked to manage a large society wedding. There are going to be thousands of guests coming from many parts of the world, lavish displays of flowers, music and entertainment, sightseers, media representatives and many other things to plan and manage. You would need a lot of help, which would involve delegating parts of the project to various experts. How would you go about breaking this project down into manageable chunks?

The WBS design is not quite as straightforward as might first be thought and there is more than one possible solution, any of which might be workable. Two of these solutions are shown in part in Figure 6.4. In both cases only the first level of breakdown is shown, and some work packages have been left out because of lack of space (for example, preparation of invitations and the gift request list). However, the diagrams in Figure 6.4 are adequate for the purposes of illustration. Remember that the aim of the WBS is to break the project down into bits that can be assigned to different managers or people in a logical way.

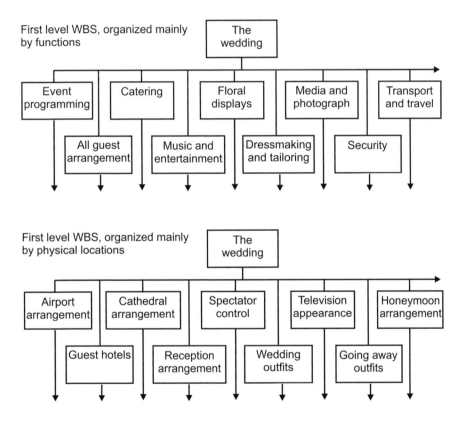

6.4   Alternative WBS patterns for a large wedding project

In the upper WBS of Figure 6.4 it is assumed that a different manager will be engaged for each specialist function. For example, a music and entertainments organizer will be expected to choose the music for the wedding ceremony in the cathedral and also engage performers for the reception event. The person organizing the floral displays will be expected to provide these inside the cathedral, at possible external locations, and at the reception. One important role is the security manager and he or she will have responsibility for security at all venues connected with this wedding.

Now consider the lower of the two WBS patterns given in Figure 6.4. Here the major work packages have been determined primarily by the location of the tasks involved. Thus the person responsible for airport arrangements will organize meeting guests at the airport and possibly also transporting them to their hotels, but a different manager will book the guests' hotel accommodation. One manager is responsible for all the cathedral arrangements, including the order of service, music, flower arrangements, seating plan and security.

The functional solution shown in the upper Figure 6.4 diagram is probably more cost-effective and tends to place top level tasks in the hands of fewer managers and, moreover, managers who should have the essential technical or operational skills. However, some people might prefer the WBS in the bottom half of Figure 6.4.

Thus there are projects where more than one acceptable WBS pattern can be found.

CODING SYSTEMS

General

Every project task will need to be given a name or descriptive title, but such names must always be augmented by a specific code. Names usually describe the nature of the task (for example, dig hole, paint door, install and test new server, and so on) but these names do not usually indicate where the task lies with respect to the work breakdown or, indeed, within the physical layout of that finished project. One difficulty with descriptive names is the limited space often causes them to be abbreviated in schedules, so that 'test customer billing system' might be reduced to 'test cust bill' where column space is limited in a schedule or report.

It is essential that every task be given some short tag that identifies it accurately, uniquely and, at the same time, indicates its exact position in the WBS hierarchy. Codes can do that.

A code may be a sequence of alphabetic characters, a set of numerical digits, or some mix of these two (an alphanumeric code). Coding systems should be designed so that the maximum amount of information about each item is conveyed by the minimum possible number of characters.

The designer of a project management coding system must always bear in mind that it should not be treated in isolation from other management and engineering information systems in the same organization. There are many advantages to applying a common coding system over all projects and other activities in a company. Suitable design will enable the same system to be used for all departments, so that codes relate costs, budgets, document numbers and the physical components of projects.

Functions of Code

A code is a short and precise method for conveying essential data about an item. For project management purposes an item can be anything from the whole project to the smallest part of it, physical or abstract. It could be a component, a drawing, a task, a human skill – anything, in fact, that is necessary for the project.

One thing that most of these coded items have in common is that they are associated with cost. Each item (either by itself or grouped with others) has costs that must be estimated, budgeted, spent, measured, reported, assessed and (where appropriate) recovered. So identification codes are also likely to be used as cost codes.

Codes used in applications are familiar and essential in computer systems for filing and data processing. The code for any particular item will perform the first of the following functions and possibly one or both of the others listed below:

1. A code must act as a unique name that *identifies* the item to which it refers.
2. The identifying code, either by itself or by the addition of subcodes, can be arranged so that it categorizes, qualifies, or in some other way *describes* the item to which it relates.
3. A code can act as an address – postcodes are an obvious example. Bin numbers used in stores and warehouses are another. And, of course, codes identify computer files.

The best coding systems are those which manage to combine these functions as simply as possible in numbers that can be used throughout a company's management information system.

Examples follow that show the kind of information which can be contained within the code for any item. The systems used as examples here and illustrated in Figures 6.5, 6.6, 6.7 and 6.8 are taken from projects in my own experience, but the general principles apply to all projects.

Coded WBS for a Radiocommunications Project

Figure 6.5 is a work breakdown structure for a small radiocommunications project, to which codes have been added, as follows:

- Project identifier – the project identification number for the breakdown shown in Figure 6.5 is 110-000. This number is sufficient to identify the project for all accounting, engineering and manufacturing purposes. Such project numbers are typically allocated from a register. Some companies might call them contract numbers or works order numbers instead. It is possible to design the project numbering method so that each number gives key information about its project, in addition to acting as a simple identifier. Examples of this also occur in Figures 6.7 and 6.8.

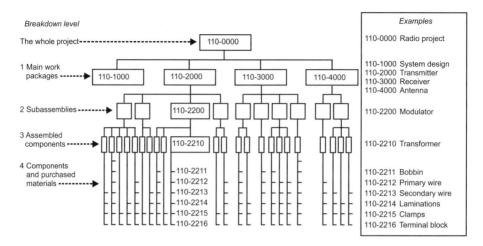

6.5   Part of the WBS and coding structure for a radiocommunications project

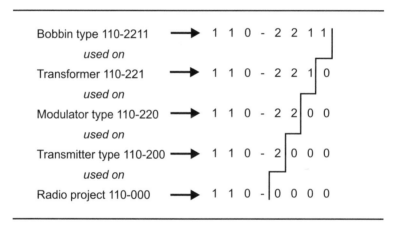

6.6   Detail from the radiocommunications project WBS

- Item identifier – each number, provided it is unique within the system, is an unambiguous way of naming any item. It is easy, however, to transpose digits or make other errors when entering numbers on forms or keyboards. It is wise, therefore, to bracket a concise description with the number whenever possible as a simple precaution against undiscovered numerical errors. Thus it is usually better to refer to an item as 'Transformer 110-221' in documents than just '110-221'.
- Relationship within the project – further examination of Figure 6.5 shows that the code numbers have been designed to correspond with the WBS hierarchy. Examples are given for components of the Transformer 110-221 and set out

more clearly in Figure 6.6. The codes denote that all numbers starting with the string 110 are used on Project 110-000, and further that numbers starting 110-221 are used on Transformer 110-221.

- Operation identifier – the task of winding the purpose-built transformer 110-221 might be given a related cost code, such as 110-221C, where the C suffix denotes the coil winding operation. A two-digit suffix is more likely to be used than a single letter, allowing greater scope for detailed breakdown into several individual operations.

- Identifier for department, discipline or trade and labour grade – a one- or two-digit subcode is often incorporated to show which department is responsible for a particular item. More digits can be added to denote the trade or engineering discipline involved. Consider, for instance, the activity of designing Transformer 110-221. The complete cost code might be 110-221-153 with the three-digit subcode 153 in this case showing that the engineering department (1) is responsible for the task, the engineering discipline is electrical (coded 5), and the last digit (3) indicates the standard cost grade of the person expected to do the task.

Two Examples of Coding Systems for Larger Projects

Figure 6.7 shows the codes used by a heavy engineering company for the work breakdown structures of all its multi-million pound projects. Figure 6.8 shows the WBS codes used by a mining engineering company for projects that could cost billions of pounds. Both examples have proved very practicable in all respects.

BENEFITS OF A LOGICAL CODING SYSTEM

Without coded information in a database, something akin to chaos would reign in all but the smallest project because of the multiple flows of data. Coding facilitates collection and redistribution of data throughout a project organization. These states of order and chaos are illustrated in Figure 6.9.

Although the primary purpose of a coding system might be to identify tasks and parts or to allocate costs, there are many benefits for the company which can maintain a logical coding system where all the codes and subcodes have common significance throughout the company's management information systems. These benefits increase with time and the accrual of records, provided that the system is used consistently without unauthorized adaptations or additions.

The benefits depend on being able to retrieve and process the data effectively. If a coding system is designed logically (taking account of hierarchical structure and families) and is well managed, some or all of the following benefits can be expected:

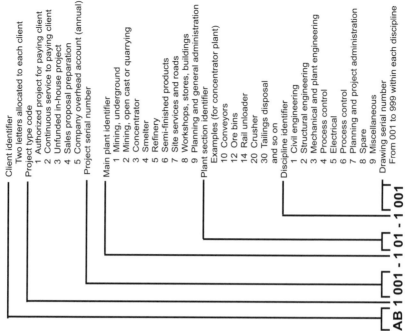

6.8 Codes used by a mining engineering company

AB 1 001 - 1 01 - 1 001

- Client identifier
  - Two letters allocated to each client
- Project type code
  - 1 Authorized project for paying client
  - 2 Continuous service to paying client
  - 3 Unfunded in-house project
  - 4 Sales proposal preparation
  - 5 Company overhead account (annual)
- Project serial number
- Main plant identifier
  - 1 Mining, underground
  - 2 Mining, open cast or quarrying
  - 3 Concentrator
  - 4 Smelter
  - 5 Refinery
  - 6 Semi-finished products
  - 7 Site services and roads
  - 8 Workshops, stores, buildings
  - 9 Planning and general administration
- Plant section identifier
  - Examples (for concentrator plant)
  - 10 Conveyors
  - 12 Ore bins
  - 14 Rail unloader
  - 20 Crusher
  - 30 Tailings disposal
  - and so on
- Discipline identifier
  - 1 Civil engineering
  - 2 Structural engineering
  - 3 Mechanical and plant engineering
  - 4 Process control
  - 5 Electrical
  - 6 Process control
  - 7 Planning and project administration
  - 8 Spare
  - 9 Miscellaneous
- Drawing serial number
  - From 001 to 999 within each discipline

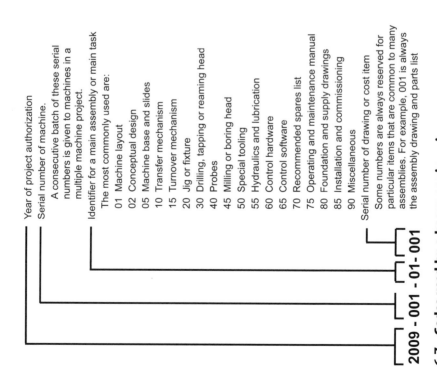

6.7 Codes used by a heavy engineering company

2009 - 001 - 01- 001

- Year of project authorization
- Serial number of machine.
  - A consecutive batch of these serial numbers is given to machines in a multiple machine project.
- Identifier for a main assembly or main task
  - The most commonly used are:
  - 01 Machine layout
  - 02 Conceptual design
  - 05 Machine base and slides
  - 10 Transfer mechanism
  - 15 Turnover mechanism
  - 20 Jig or fixture
  - 30 Drilling, tapping or reaming head
  - 40 Probes
  - 45 Milling or boring head
  - 50 Special tooling
  - 55 Hydraulics and lubrication
  - 60 Control hardware
  - 65 Control software
  - 70 Recommended spares list
  - 75 Operating and maintenance manual
  - 80 Foundation and supply drawings
  - 85 Installation and commissioning
  - 90 Miscellaneous
- Serial number of drawing or cost item
  - Some numbers are always reserved for particular items that are common to many assemblies. For example, 001 is always the assembly drawing and parts list

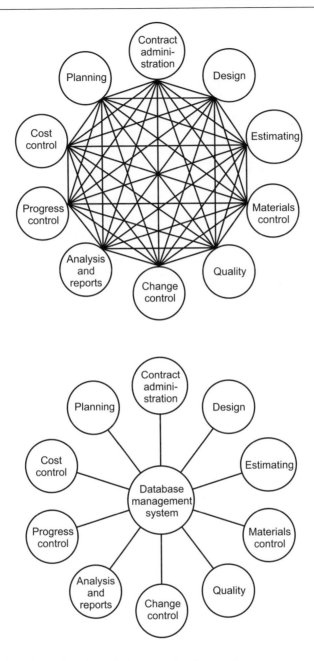

6.9 Coded data in a database brings order from chaos

- Easy retrieval of items from records of past projects which correspond to or are similar to items expected in new projects, essential as a basis for making comparative cost estimates.
- Easy search and retrieval of design information (especially flowsheets, calculations and drawings) for processes, assemblies or components used on past projects which are relevant to a current project. This 'retained engineering' can save considerable engineering design work, time and costs if all or part of the previous design can be re-used or adapted. Not only does such design retrieval avoid the unnecessary costs of designing everything afresh, it also allows the new project to incorporate designs that have already been proven or debugged, so that the scope for errors is reduced.
- Rapid identification of purchase requisitions and specifications from previous projects for equipment which corresponds to new equipment requirements. One application of this is to speed the preparation of new purchase specifications, particularly when much or all of the previous text can be used again.
- Grouping of components into families according to their basic shapes and sizes. This is particularly necessary for manufacturing operations where the plant is arranged in cells for group technology.
- If it is possible to use a common system, then the cost estimates, budgets, recorded costs, drawing schedules, many other documents, and tasks on the project plan can all be related in a database for project administration, management reports and control.
- The ability to carry out statistical analyses on cost records and other documents from past projects for a variety of reasons, including monitoring performance trends.

The following examples from my experience had great practical use in a heavy engineering company, and illustrate only two of the many possibilities for exploiting properly coded records:

1. The averaging of recorded costs for commonly recurring work packages in a range of categories from many past projects. This led to the preparation of project estimating tables (expressed in man-hours and updated materials costs). These tables proved very useful for planning and resource scheduling new projects and for making global checks on detailed estimates for new project proposals.
2. Analysis in detail of past shipping records enabled a table to be compiled that listed all the main components commonly produced in the company's very heavy engineering projects. For each item it was possible to forecast the most likely average and the maximum weight of each part of the project after it had been broken down into parts of 20 tonnes or less for shipping. Cost estimates were added with the help of a shipping company. The result was given to the materials control manager as a 'ready-reckoner'. With occasional updating, this table was used successfully for estimating future project shipping costs to all parts of the world.

CHOOSING A CODING SYSTEM

Once a coding system has become well established it is difficult and unwise to make any fundamental change. Any comprehensive system has, therefore, to be designed with a great deal of care, so that it will serve the organization well into the future. Suppose that a company has been operating for many years with a comprehensive arrangement of codes that are recognized by its management information systems. Suppose, further, that this same arrangement of codes is common to many procedures and tasks. Then, for example, the number for the drawing of a manufactured component would also be used as (or would be a recognizable constituent of) related manufacturing job numbers, job cost records and the stock and part number of the component itself. If this company were to make a change to the numbering system, so that numbers which previously had one meaning would denote something entirely different in the future, some of the following problems might arise:

1. Drawings filed under two different systems;
2. Similar inconvenience caused to long-standing customers who maintain their own files of project drawings;
3. No easy way of identifying similar previous jobs for the purpose of comparative cost estimating;
4. Difficulty in retrieving earlier designs. The opportunity to use retained engineering from past work to reduce future design effort might be lost;
5. Staff must live with two different systems instead of one universal set of numbers;
6. Problems for storekeepers and stock controllers, with more than one part numbering method – parts common to earlier projects may have to be renumbered for newer projects, so that there is a possibility of having identical common parts stored in two places with different part numbers;
7. Mayhem created in any attempt to use a relational database that relies on code numbering.

The Need for Simplicity

This is the place to insert a word of warning. It is tempting to be too ambitious and try to make numbers include too much information. The result can be codes that contain 14, 15 or more characters. It is easy to fall into such a trap, especially when the system is designed by a committee, each of whose members contributes their own idea of what the numbers might be expected to denote. Beware of phrases such as 'Wouldn't it be nice if...'.

The designer of a system that depends on exceptionally long codes may feel very proud of their system's capability. Computer systems are well able to accept and process huge numbers, but please remember the human element — the 'people interface'. People will have to work with these numbers, entering them in written or electronic records. Barcodes can help, but I remember an attempt to introduce a very complex coding system on a mine development project in a remote area of Australia. The system designer was a highly qualified and well-respected member of the London head office management staff. Supervisors, professional people and artisans at the mine were all expected to read and write 18-digit job codes on documents without making mistakes while exposed to unpleasant and hazardous conditions both above and below ground. The people at the mine never even attempted to use the codes. Even if they had used them, the depth of information that the codes contained was far in excess of that needed for management information. Simple codes use less effort and result in fewer errors. Remember the old and sensible slogan KISS: **K**eep **i**t **S**imple, **S**tupid.

WHAT HAPPENS WHEN THE CUSTOMER SAYS 'YOU SHALL USE MY CODING SYSTEM!'?

An irritating problem often arises when a customer insists that their own numbering system is used, rather than project contractor's own long-established and proven arrangement. This happens, for example, when a project customer is to be presented with a complete set of project drawings as part of the contract and wants to be able to file these along with all the other drawings in the customer's system. This, unfortunately, is a case where 'the customer is always right'.

This problem of having to use customers' codes is not always restricted to drawings. In some projects it can apply to equipment numbers or part numbers. It also occurs, and is a great nuisance, in the cost codes used for work packages or large purchases for major projects. The customer and contractor sometimes work together to plan, authorize and arrange the release of funds (either from the customer's own resources or from an external financing organization). In such cases the customer might insist that all estimates, budgets and subsequent cost reports for the project are broken down against the customer's own capital appropriation or other cost codes.

Three Options

There are three possible options when the customer asks the contractor to use a 'foreign' coding system.

Option 1: say 'No!' to the customer

This option is either courageous or foolhardy. It might even be impossible under the terms of contract. In any case, it would be a shortcut to achieving bad customer relations or losing the customer altogether.

Option 2: change over completely to the customer's system

With this option, the contractor calls the project a 'special case', abandons the in-house system, asks the customer for a set of their own procedures, and uses those for the project. This option is difficult for the following reasons:

- Data retrieval and comparison with other projects would be impossible for this project.
- It will soon be discovered that every project is a 'special case'. The contractor might soon be using as many coding systems as there are customers.

Option 3: use both systems simultaneously

This option, the sensible compromise course, offers a practical solution. Every drawing and other affected item must be numbered twice, once for each system.

Everything must, of course, be diligently cross-referenced between the two systems. This sounds tedious and time-consuming and means that staff have to learn more than one system. At one time this would have added significant time and costs to a project, but now a computer database can take the strain.

7 *Planning the Timescale*

Whenever any job has to be finished within a time deadline, it is advisable to have some idea of the relationship between the time needed and the time available. This is true for any project, whether a dinner is being prepared or a motorway constructed. In the first case one would be ill advised to tell guests 'Dinner is at seven – but the potatoes will not be ready until 7.30'. Similarly, there would be little point in having an eminent person arrive to open a new motorway if, by cutting the tape, the unsuspecting traffic were to be freed to rush headlong towards an unfinished bridge that comprised a few girders over a yawning chasm, complete with rushing torrent below. A plan will always be needed if a project is to be finished on time. In our culinary example planning is simple and informal, conducted solely within the brain of the cook. Projects such as motorways are more complicated and need special techniques.

This chapter begins by explaining bar charts, which can be adequate for planning and progressing small projects. They are also particularly useful during the early phases of even very large projects, when there is not enough information about the tasks that lie ahead to allow more detailed planning.

BAR CHARTS

Bar charts are also widely known as Gantt charts, after their originator, the American industrial engineer Henry Gantt (1861–1919). They have long been in widespread use and are valuable planning aids. Anyone who can understand an office holiday chart can draw and understand a project bar chart.

The visual impact of a bar chart can be a powerful aid to controlling a project. Bar charts are preferred to other methods by many senior managers because they need no specialist training to understand them. All levels of supervision and management find them convenient as day-to-day control tools. Even when projects have been planned with more advanced methods, the computer systems (such as Microsoft Project) are often used to convert the schedules into bar charts for day-to-day use.

Bar charts are drawn to scale, with the horizontal axis directly proportional to time. Days, months, years or other units are used, chosen to suit the overall duration of the project. Each horizontal bar represents a project task, with its length scaled according to its expected duration. The name or description of each job is written on the same row as its bar, usually at the left-hand edge.

A Bar Chart Case Example: the Furniture Project

Eaton Sitright Limited is a company that manufactures furniture. The company wishes to introduce a new table and chair to its standard range and has a project to design and make a small prototype batch for consumer appraisal and testing. The furniture will be steel framed, and the table is to be provided with one drawer. Figure 7.1 lists the main tasks for this project. The extreme right-hand column lists, for each task, the immediately preceding tasks that must be completed before the new task can start.

Activity number	Activity description	Duration (days)	Preceding activities
	Chair		
01	Anatomical study for chair	15	None
02	Design chair	5	01
03	Buy materials for chair seat	6	02
04	Make chair seat	3	03
05	Buy chair castors	5	02
06	Buy steel for chair frame	10	02
07	Make chair frame	3	06
08	Paint chair frame	2	07, 21
09	Assemble chair	1	04, 05, 08
10	Apply final finishes to chair	2	09
	Desk		
11	Design desk	10	None
12	Buy steel for desk frame	10	11
13	Make desk frame	5	12, 15
14	Paint desk frame	2	13, 21
15	Buy wood and fittings for desk	5	15
16	Make desk drawer	6	15
17	Make desk top	1	15
18	Assemble desk	1	14, 16, 17
19	Apply final finishes to desk	2	18
	General activities		
20	Decide paint colours	10	None
21	Buy paint and varnish	8	20
22	Final project evaluation	5	10, 19

7.1 Task list for the furniture project

Figure 7.2 is the resulting bar chart. The planner has tried to observe the dependencies given in the final column of the task list. For example, the paint colours must be decided before paint can be purchased. No painting task can start before the relevant article has been manufactured and the paint has been purchased. Although bar charts cannot show such relationships, these can be dealt with mentally on this simple project. With a larger project, however, there would be a considerable risk of producing a chart containing some logical impossibilities.

Task ID and description	Day number																					
	2	4	6	8	10	12	14	16	18	20	22	24	26	28	30	32	34	36	38	40	42	44
01 Anatomical study for chair	■	■	■	■	■	■	■															
02 Design chair								■	■	■												
03 Buy materials for chair seat										■	■	■										
04 Make chair seat														■	■							
05 Buy chair castors										■	■	■										
06 Buy steel for chair frame										■	■	■	■									
07 Make chair frame																■	■					
08 Paint chair frame																	■					
09 Assemble chair																		■				
10 Apply final finishes to chair																			■	■		
11 Design desk		■	■	■																		
12 Buy steel for desk frame							■	■	■	■												
13 Make desk frame										■	■	■										
14 Paint desk frame												■	■									
15 Buy wood and fittings for desk						■	■	■														
16 Make desk drawer							■	■	■													
17 Make desk top						■																
18 Assemble desk													■									
19 Apply final finishes to desk													■	■								
20 Decide paint colours		■	■	■																		
21 Buy paint and varnish						■	■	■														
22 Final project evaluation																				■	■	■

7.2 Bar chart (or Gantt chart) for the furniture project

Link lines can be added to bar charts to indicate dependencies (logical constraints) between two or more jobs. Figure 7.3 is a linked version of the bar chart of Figure 7.2. This shows clearly, for example, that the chair design cannot start before the anatomical study has been completed. Even for this tiny project, however, the linked bar chart cannot show every task dependency without becoming difficult to follow. It would be difficult to draw the links from 'Buy paint and varnish' to the starts of the two painting jobs without producing crossovers and some confusion (although, in this simple case, these particular crossovers could be eliminated by listing the tasks in a different sequence). Many project management computer applications are capable of plotting linked bar charts, but the results are usually cluttered and difficult to interpret except for small projects.

This furniture project will be revisited later in this chapter to see how much more effective it would be for the Eaton Sitright company to plan its project with a critical path network.

Task ID and description	Day number
	2 4 6 8 10 12 14 16 18 20 22 24 26 28 30 32 34 36 38 40 42 44
01 Anatomical study for chair	
02 Design chair	
03 Buy materials for chair seat	
04 Make chair seat	
05 Buy chair castors	
06 Buy steel for chair frame	
07 Make chair frame	
08 Paint chair frame	
09 Assemble chair	
10 Apply final finishes to chair	
11 Design desk	
12 Buy steel for desk frame	
13 Make desk frame	
14 Paint desk frame	
15 Buy wood and fittings for desk	
16 Make desk drawer	
17 Make desk top	
18 Assemble desk	
19 Apply final finishes to desk	
20 Decide paint colours	
21 Buy paint and varnish	
22 Final project evaluation	

7.3 Linked bar chart for the furniture project

Bar Charts as Progress Monitoring Aids

Bar charts can be used to plot progress. For this purpose a date cursor can be added, which is a vertical line placed on the chart at the review date. In project planning, a review date is often called 'time-now'. If the bar chart is drawn or printed on paper, the cursor can be formed by placing a straight edge or ruler vertically on the chart at the time-now date. In the past, a vertical scarlet cord or ribbon was used on an adjustable wall-mounted bar chart to show time-now. Those wallcharts have now fallen into disuse, replaced by one of the many available computer applications.

Whatever method is used to prepare and display the bar chart, progress assessment is simply a matter of checking that all tasks (or portions of tasks) lying to the left of the date cursor have been completed. This highlights all tasks that are running late.

Bar Chart Limitations

The inability of bar charts to depict clearly the dependencies between different tasks has been demonstrated, but bar charts have other limitations. For example, when a chart shows a large number of tasks over many days (or other periods) it is difficult to trace individual tasks along the rows and columns.

Although it is possible to schedule more than 100 jobs using a hand-drawn chart or wall planner, rescheduling is a different story. Setting up a complex plan in the first place might take a few working days but adjusting it subsequently to keep in step with changes is very difficult and time-consuming.

Colour coding can be used on charts to indicate different types of tasks or resource needs, but the visual effectiveness of a chart is lost when too many colour codes are introduced.

CRITICAL PATH ANALYSIS

The origins of critical path networks can be traced back to several different sources, even before the Second World War, but it was in the US during the 1950s that they were fully exploited. They became more popular in the 1960s when suitable computer systems became available to remove the drudgery of scheduling and (particularly) rescheduling.

Network diagrams show all the logical interdependencies between different jobs. The planner can ensure, for example, that bricklaying will never be scheduled to start before its supporting foundations are ready. Such mistakes are easily possible with complex bar charts, where it is impossible to depict or see every logical constraint.

Another great strength of networks is that they allow priorities to be quantified, based on an analysis of all the task duration estimates. Those tasks that cannot be delayed without endangering project completion on time are identified as critical tasks, and all other tasks can be ranked according their degree of criticality.

Networks cannot be used directly for resource scheduling. In this respect bar charts are superior and easier to understand, provided that the number of activities is very small. However, networks assign time-based priorities to tasks and highlight critical jobs, which is a vital contribution to the resource scheduling process (resource scheduling is described in Chapter 8). Most project management software can schedule resources.

Even if no duration estimates are made and there is no time analysis, the benefits derived from drawing a network can be worthwhile. Networking encourages logical thinking. A planning meeting can be regarded as a productive form of brainstorming. A network diagram shows clearly interactivity dependencies and relationships. The process of drawing a network can highlight activities that might otherwise have been forgotten, and thus excluded from schedules, estimates, cost budgets and pricing.

TWO DIFFERENT NETWORK NOTATION SYSTEMS

Several network systems were devised during the second half of the twentieth century, but these all fit within one or other of two principal groups:

1. Activity-on-arrow networks, often called arrow networks or ADM (short for arrow diagrams) or less commonly activity-on-arrow (AoA).
2. Precedence networks, also known as PDM (short for precedence diagrams) or activity-on-node (AoN) networks.

Arrow networks are faster and easier to draw (and erase and redraw) than their precedence counterparts. That can save valuable time at initial planning meetings, which are invariably attended by busy senior people. But precedence networks are better suited to computer processing. If a planner chooses to sketch a first draft network in arrow notation, it is a simple matter to convert it to precedence notation later for the computer. Most computer applications only use precedence notation but Micro Planner X-Pert is capable of processing both arrow and precedence networks competently.

Arrow networks are described briefly in the following section, but most of the examples in this book will be given using the precedence system because this is far more widely used.

Although precedence diagrams are not as well-suited as arrow diagrams for rapid sketching on paper, it is fairly easy to draw and edit them on the computer screen. However, the limited screen area available when compared with a roll of drawing paper means that larger network diagrams require much tedious scrolling up, down and sideways. It is not possible to see the whole picture and trace long paths through a network with an index finger or pointer unless the network is drawn or printed on a large area of paper.

CRITICAL PATH NETWORKS USING ARROW DIAGRAMS

Explanations given here are repeated in the precedence diagram section that follows. Thus readers can skip this arrow diagram section if they are only interested in using the precedence method.

Activities and Events in Arrow Diagrams

Figure 7.4 is a simple arrow diagram. Each circle denotes a project *event*, such as the start of work or the completion of an activity. The arrow joining any two events represents the *activity* or *task* that must take place before the second event can be declared as achieved. The terms *task* and *activity* usually have the same meaning nowadays. Thus in Figure 7.4 eleven activities link six events (ignore the dotted arrow for the time being).

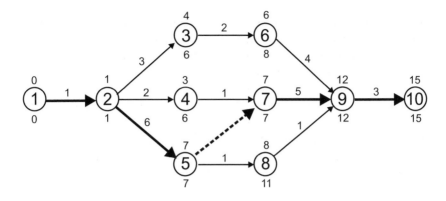

7.4   The elements of an arrow critical path network diagram

All network diagrams are drawn so that work progresses from left to right. They are not drawn to scale and neither the lengths of the arrows nor the spacing of events have any significance.

The numbers in the event circles label the events. They allow the events and their associated activities to be referred to without ambiguity. Thus the arrow from event 1 to event 2 can be described as activity 1-2. Such numbering is essential for processing arrow networks by computer.

The logical significance of the diagram in Figure 7.4 is that each event cannot be considered achieved until all the activities leading into it have been finished. Only then, and not before, can activities immediately following the event be started.

The dotted arrow in Figure 7.4 is a dummy activity. Dummy activities (called dummies for short) do not represent work and almost always have zero duration. Instead, they denote a constraint or line of dependence between different events. In this case, therefore, the start of activity 7-9 is dependent not only upon completion of activity 4-7, but must also await completion of activity 2-5. Alternatively expressed, activity 7-9 cannot start until events 5 and 7 have both been achieved.

In practice, each arrow on a real project network would have its task name or description written along the length of the arrow. Lack of space in diagrams and computer report columns means that these activity descriptions are usually kept short, sometimes even abbreviated to the extent that they are barely intelligible.

Time Analysis

Numbers have been written above the activity arrows in Figure 7.4 to show their estimated durations. The units are chosen as being the most suitable for the project. Once chosen, the same time units must be used consistently throughout any network. Assume that the numbers in this illustration are weeks. These estimates are strictly for *duration* only, which means *elapsed time*, not necessarily the work content. In fact, for some 'activities' (such as procurement lead times) there might be no work content for the project staff at all.

The first purpose of time analysis is to determine the shortest possible time in which a project can be finished, taking into account all the logical constraints and activity duration estimates. It is not usual to take resource allocation into account at this stage because that problem can be resolved at a later stage (described in Chapter 8).

Time analysis also performs the vital function of determining which activities should be given the most priority. This is achieved by calculating a quantity called float, which is the amount by which any activity can be allowed to slip past its earliest possible start and finish dates without delaying the whole project.

The forward pass

In the network of Figure 7.4, the earliest project duration possible has been calculated by adding the activity duration estimates along the arrows from left to right. This is always the first step in the full time analysis of any network and is known as the 'forward pass'.

The forward pass additions will depend on which path is followed. The earliest possible completion time for event 7, for instance might seem to be 1 + 2 + 1 = 4, if the path through events 1, 2, 4 and 7 is taken. However, event 7 cannot be achieved until event 5 has also been achieved, because of the link through the dummy. The path through events 1, 2, 5 and the dummy is the longer of the two possible paths and that must, therefore, determine the earliest possible time for the achievement of event 7. Thus the earliest possible time for event 7 is the end of week 7 (1 + 6). This means also that the earliest possible start time for activity 7-9 is the end of week 7 (which in practical terms means the beginning of week 8).

The earliest possible time for an event (and therefore the earliest possible start time for its immediately succeeding activities) is found by adding the estimates of all activities along the path leading into it. When there is more than one path, the one with the highest total time estimate must be chosen. By continuing this process through the network to the end of the project at event 10 it emerges that the earliest possible estimated project completion time is 15 weeks.

The backward pass

Now consider event 9 in Figure 7.4. Its earliest possible achievement time is the end of week 12. It is clear that activity 8-9 could be delayed for up to three weeks beyond its earliest possible start without upsetting the overall timescale, because there are longer paths leading into event 9. In other words, although the earliest possible achievement time for event 8 is week 8, it could be delayed by up to three weeks, to the end of week 11, without delaying the earliest possible completion time for event 9. This result is indicated on the arrow diagram by writing the latest permissible time underneath the event circle. The result is found this time, not by addition from left to right along the arrows, but in exactly the opposite way by subtracting the estimated duration times from right to left (15 – 3 – 1 = 11, for event 8).

This subtraction process must be repeated throughout the network, writing the latest permissible times below all their event circles. Wherever more than one possible path exists, the longest must always be chosen so that subtraction gives the smallest remainder (the earliest time). This is illustrated for example at event 5, where the correct backwards subtraction route lies through the dummy (15 – 3 – 5 = 7). The path through events 10, 9, 8, and 5 is shorter and would give the incorrect answer 15 – 3 – 1 – 1 = 10, which would be 3 days too late. Event 5 must be achieved by the end of week 7, not 10, if the project is to finish on time.

The earliest and latest times written above and below the event circles also apply to the activities leading into and out of the events. Thus, for example, activity 8-9 has the following time analysis data:

- Estimated duration: 1 week
- Earliest possible start: end of week 8 (effectively the beginning of week 9)
- Earliest possible finish (8 + 1): end of week 9
- Latest permissible finish: end of week 12
- Total float: 3 weeks

Float and the critical path

The term 'float' indicates the amount of leeway available for starting and finishing an activity without the project end date being affected. Total float is the difference between the earliest and latest start times for any activity (or between its earliest and latest finish times). There are other categories of float, explained in Chapter 8, but they can be ignored for all the examples in this chapter.

When all the earliest possible and latest permissible event times have been added to the diagram, there will always be at least one chain of events that each have the same earliest and latest times, indicating zero float. These events are critical to the successful achievement of the whole project within its earliest possible time. The route joining these events is not surprisingly termed the 'critical path'.

Although all activities may be important, it is the critical activities (the activities that form the critical path or paths) that must claim greatest priority for scarce resources and management attention.

PRECEDENCE NETWORK DIAGRAMS

This section repeats some of the text from the previous section for the benefit of readers who skipped the explanation of arrow networks.

A precedence diagram must be constructed with careful thought to ensure that it shows as accurately as possible the logical relationships and interdependencies of each activity or task with all the others in the project.

Activities (or tasks)

Figure 7.5 shows the notation commonly used for an activity in precedence notation. The simple precedence network in Figure 7.6 is the precedence equivalent of the arrow diagram in Figure 7.4. The numbers in brackets in each activity box in Figure 7.6 indicate the equivalent arrows in Figure 7.4.

The flow of work in any network diagram is from left to right. Precedence diagrams are not drawn to scale and neither the length of links nor the size of the activity boxes have any significance whatsoever. Every activity is given a unique ID code. These codes are essential for computer processing. ID codes can range from small serial numbers to complex alphanumeric codes containing 10 or even more characters, depending on the size and complexity of the networks, the nature of the projects being planned and the capabilities of the computer software.

The activities (tasks) comprising a project are joined by arrows which, unlike those in arrow diagrams, simply represent constraints or links. Because all arrows travel from left to right, we usually leave out the arrowheads.

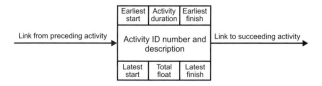

7.5 An activity in precedence notation

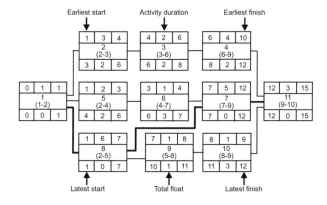

7.6 The elements of a precedence critical path network diagram

Dummy activities are rarely needed in precedence networks. When they are used, they have zero duration and do not denote work but are occasionally included in a network to clarify logic or tidy up the drawing. For example, it is usually convenient to create artificial start and finish activities for the network. Networks that have several starts and several finishes will be found untidy for time analysis and computer processing. However, dummy start and finish activities were not needed for the network in Figure 7.6, because that network already has only one start and one finish.

Time Analysis of Precedence Networks

The units used for estimated activity durations are chosen by the planner as being the most suitable for the project. Once chosen, the same time units must be used consistently throughout any network. Assume that the numbers in Figure 7.6 are weeks. These estimates are for duration only, which means elapsed time, not necessarily the work content. In fact, for some activities (such as procurement lead times) there might be no work content for the project staff at all.

The first purpose of time analysis is to determine the shortest possible time in which a project can be completed, taking into account all the logical constraints and activity duration estimates. It is not usual to take possible shortage of resources into account at this stage because that problem is resolved at a later stage (see Chapter 8).

Time analysis also performs the vital function of determining which activities should be given the most priority. This is achieved by calculating a quantity called float, which is the amount by which any activity can be allowed to slip past its earliest possible start date without delaying the whole project.

The forward pass

In the project network of Figure 7.6, the earliest overall project duration possible has been calculated by adding activity duration estimates along the various paths, through all the links, passing from left to right. There is more than one possible path through the network and the result will obviously depend on which path is followed. The earliest possible start time for activity 7, for instance, would seem to be $1 + 2 + 1 = 4$ (the end of week 4) if the path through activities 1, 5 and 6 is taken. However, activity 7 cannot really start until the end of week 7 (which in practical terms means the beginning of week 8) because it is constrained by the longer path through activities 1 and 8 ($1 + 6 = 7$ weeks).

Thus the earliest possible start time for any activity is found by adding the times of all preceding activities along the longest path in the network. By following this procedure through the network to the end of the project at activity 11 it emerges that the earliest possible estimated project duration is 15 weeks.

The backward pass

Now consider activity 10 in Figure 7.6. Its earliest possible start time is the end of week 8. This activity has an estimated duration of 1 week and its earliest possible completion time is therefore at the end of week 9. But the following activity 11 cannot start until the end of week 12, because of longer forward paths through the network. Thus activity 10 could be delayed by 3 weeks without delaying activity 11. The start and finish times for activity 10 therefore have a float (or slack) of 3 weeks.

A backward pass through the network can determine the latest permissible times at which each activity must start and finish if the project is to finish at its earliest possible time. Contrary to the forward pass, the backward pass process means subtracting the duration of each activity from its latest permissible finish time to arrive at its latest permissible start time. This backward pass must begin at the very end of the final activity in the network diagram, and at each subsequent activity it is the path with the longest combined duration (from the right) that must be chosen.

For example, the longest path to the right of activity 8 runs through activities 7 and 11. The latest permissible finish time for activity 8 is thus 15 – 3 – 5, which is 7. As this backward pass is continued throughout the network, the other quantities along the bottoms of the activity boxes can be filled in. The latest permissible start of each activity is its latest permissible finish, minus its estimated duration.

The total float of each activity is found either by subtracting its earliest possible finish from its latest permissible finish (the same result can be obtained by subtracting the earliest possible start from the latest permissible start).

The critical path

When all the earliest possible and latest permissible times have been added to the diagram, there will be at least one chain of activities where the earliest and latest times are the same, indicating zero float. These activities are critical to the successful achievement of the whole project within its earliest possible time. The route joining these activities is not surprisingly termed the 'critical path'. Although all activities may be important, it is the critical activities that must claim priority for scarce resources and management attention.

PLANNING THE FURNITURE PROJECT BY CRITICAL PATH NETWORK

Earlier in this chapter it was shown that bar charts are very limited in their ability to show the constraints between interdependent activities. The linked bar chart in Figure 7.3 could not show all the links clearly, even for the simple furniture project carried out by the Eaton Sitright company.

Figure 7.7 shows how the furniture project plan looks as an arrow diagram and Figure 7.8 is the equivalent precedence diagram. Time analysis data are shown in both cases and the critical path is highlighted by the bold lines. These time analysis results are tabulated (for both the arrow and precedence diagrams) in Figure 7.9.

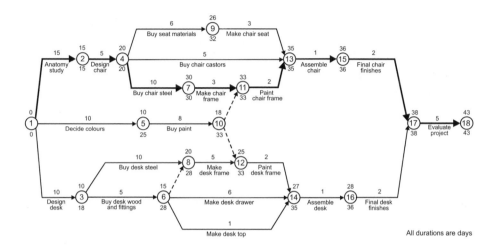

7.7   Furniture project: activity-on-arrow network diagram

The data in Figure 7.9 are all in terms of day numbers, which have little practical use for the project manager, who needs calendar dates. Conversion to calendar dates must wait until the project start date has been established. Then, computer processing of the network will automatically produce schedules with calendar dates, with holidays and weekends allowed for.

The table of data resulting from network time analysis should be of far more use to the manager of this project than any bar chart because it is not necessary to find times by scaling the chart. Also, the relative priorities of the different tasks are clearly stated in terms of their total float.

LEVEL OF DETAIL IN NETWORK DIAGRAMS

A question often facing inexperienced planners is 'How much detail should we show in the network?' In other words, which activities should be included in the network and which should be left out or combined with others?

To some extent this depends on the size of the project, the project duration, the size of the duration units chosen, the amount of detailed knowledge available and the purpose of the network. A very detailed project network containing 10,000 activities might sound very impressive, but smaller networks are more manageable.

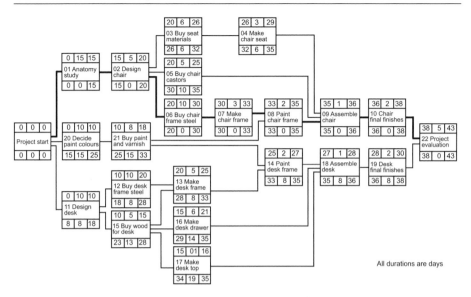

All durations are days

7.8   Furniture project: precedence network diagram

ADM only Prec. Succ. Event event		PDM Task ID	Activity description	Duration (days)	Earliest start	Latest start	Earliest finish	Latest finish	Total float
1	2	01	Anatomical study for chair	15	0	0	15	15	0
2	4	02	Design chair	5	15	15	20	20	0
4	9	03	Buy materials for chair seat	6	20	26	26	32	6
9	13	04	Make chair seat	3	26	32	29	35	6
4	13	05	Buy chair castors	5	20	30	25	35	10
4	7	06	Buy steel for chair frame	10	20	20	30	30	0
7	11	07	Make chair frame	3	30	30	33	33	0
11	13	08	Paint chair frame	2	33	33	35	35	0
13	15	09	Assemble chair	1	35	35	36	36	0
15	17	10	Apply final finishes to chair	2	36	36	38	38	0
1	3	11	Design desk	10	0	8	10	18	8
3	8	12	Buy steel for desk frame	10	10	18	20	28	8
8	12	13	Make desk frame	5	20	28	25	33	8
12	14	14	Paint desk frame	2	25	33	27	35	8
3	6	15	Buy wood and fittings for desk	5	10	23	15	28	13
6	14	16	Make desk drawer	6	15	29	21	35	14
6	14	17	Make desk top	1	15	34	16	35	19
14	16	18	Assemble desk	1	27	35	28	36	8
16	17	19	Apply final finishes to desk	2	28	36	30	38	8
1	5	20	Decide paint colours	10	0	15	10	25	15
5	10	21	Buy paint and varnish	8	10	25	18	33	15
17	18	22	Final project evaluation	5	38	38	43	43	0

7.9   Time analysis for the furniture project

Guidelines

Several guidelines apply to the level of detail which should be shown in project network diagrams.

Activities with very short durations

It is usually possible to avoid showing jobs as separate activities if their durations amount only to a very small fraction of the expected overall timescale, especially if they do not require resources. Of course these activities cannot be ignored, but they can be included in the network as parts of other activities. An example might be the preparation of a group of drawings, where a single activity 'detail and check sub-assembly X' would be shown rather than including a separate activity for detailing every drawing, and another set of activities for checking them.

As with all rules there are exceptions. Some activities with very short durations might be so important that they must be included (for example, an activity for obtaining authorization or approval before subsequent work can proceed).

In a short project lasting only a few weeks (for example, the overhaul and maintenance of an electricity generating station during a planned period of shutdown) it would be reasonable to use network planning units of days, fractions of days or even hours, and to include activities lasting only an hour or so.

Level of detail in relation to task responsibility

A network path should be broken to include a new activity whenever the action moves from one department or organization to another — in other words where the responsibility for managing the work changes. Remember that the ultimate purpose of the network is to allow the project work to be scheduled and controlled. In due course, work-to-do lists for different managers will be generated from the network. The network must contain all the jobs needed for these lists. This means that:

- No network activity should be so large that it cannot be assigned for the principal control of one, and only one department or manager.
- Activities must correspond to actions that have a clearly definable start and finish.
- The interval between the start and finish of any activity should not be too long compared with the project timescale, so that fairly frequent progress points are provided throughout the project for progress control.

A network that is sufficiently detailed will enable the following types of events to be identified, planned and monitored or measured (this example is for a manufacturing or construction project – different guidelines would apply to a management change project):

1. Work authorization, either as an internal works order or as the receipt of a customer order or contract.
2. Financial authorizations from the customer (especially where these might risk work hold-ups during the course of the project).
3. Local authority planning application and consent.
4. The start and finish of design for any subassembly. If the duration of the design task is longer than two or three weeks it might be advisable to define separate, shorter activities corresponding to design phases.
5. Release of completed drawings for production or construction (probably grouped in subassemblies or work packages rather than attempting to plan for every individual small drawing).
6. The start of purchasing activity for each subassembly or work package, signified by the engineering issue of a bill of material, purchase specification or advance release of information for items which are known to have long delivery times.
7. Issue of invitations to tender (or purchase enquiries) to suppliers.
8. Receipt and analysis of bids.
9. Following on from items 6, 7 and 8, the issue of a purchase order with a supplier or subcontractor (again at the level of work packages and subassemblies rather than small individual purchases).
10. Material deliveries, often meaning the event when the last item needed to complete the materials for a particular work package (or for a single item of capital equipment) is received on site or at the factory. For international projects, this delivery point may be to a ship or to an aircraft, with subsequent transit time shown as a separate, consecutive activity (when the change of responsibility rule applies, because responsibility transfers from the supplier to the carrier or freight forwarding agent).
11. The starts and completions of manufacturing stages (in large projects usually only looking at the entries into and exits from production control responsibility, and again considering work packages or subassemblies rather than individual small parts).
12. The starts and finishes of construction subcontracts, and important intermediate events in such subcontracts (see the section 'Milestones' below).
13. Handover activities for completed work packages. This would include activities for handing over the finished project, or major parts of it, to the customer but would also ensure that associated items such as maintenance and operating manuals were itemized separately in the network plan.

These are, of course, only guidelines. The list is intended to be neither mandatory nor complete.

Level of critical path network detail in relation to activity costs

Some cost reporting and control measures will be impossible if sufficient attention to certain activities is not given when the network diagram is prepared.

It is possible to assign a cost to an activity, such as the purchase of materials. If an activity is included on the network for the planned issue of every significant purchase order, then the purchase order cost value can be assigned to these activities. This makes possible the preparation of reports from the computer which will set the times for these costs when the orders are placed and thus give a schedule of purchase cost commitments.

If another activity is added for the receipt of goods against each of these purchase orders, the same order value can be assigned to these later activities. Using suitable computer techniques, cost schedules can then be derived that relate to the time when invoices will become due. These schedules indicate cash flow requirements.

None of this would be possible without sufficient detail on the network.

MILESTONES

It is important to provide intermediate points throughout the network and any resulting schedules that can be used as progress benchmarks. This is done by designating significant activities as 'milestones'. Computer programs for project scheduling allow reports to be filtered and printed so that they contain only such milestone activities, and these greatly help the assessment of progress against time and costs and are of value in reporting to higher management and to the customer.

IS THE PREDICTED TIMESCALE TOO LONG?

It is often found that the first forward pass through a network will predict a completion date that is unacceptably late. The planner is then likely to be placed under great pressure to come up with an alternative plan to meet the required timescale (which might correspond to a delivery promise already made to a customer).

One option is to consider spending more money in additional resources, use of overtime, or special machinery to speed up critical activities, a process sometimes called crashing. Crashing can add risk and cost to a project without adding value, and is to be avoided if possible.

The planner might be tempted to cut estimates arbitrarily, perhaps on the advice of other managers, until the work fits neatly into the timescale. That must, of course, never be considered as a valid option unless good reasons can be given as to how the shorter times will be achieved.

A more sensible first course of action is to re-examine the network logic. Are all the constraints shown really constraints? Can any activities be overlapped, so that the start dates of some critical activities are brought forward? A process called 'fast-tracking' considers the performing of activities in parallel that have traditionally been performed serially. In any case, a network should always be checked to ensure that it reflects the most practicable and efficient way of working.

Most networks use only simple start-finish relationships, but the planner should always bear in mind the availability of more complex notation in precedence systems and be prepared to use start-start or other complex links to overlap suitable activities and bring the planned completion date forward. Figure 7.10 shows the range of constraints that precedence diagramming allows. However, the finish-start relationship shown in Figure 7.10(a) is by far the most commonly used and is the default assumed by computer programs.

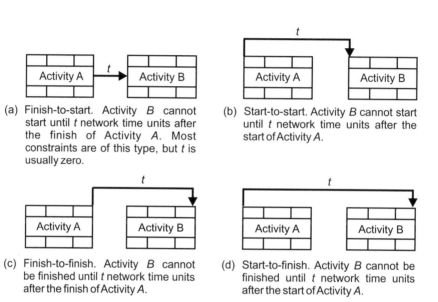

(a) Finish-to-start. Activity *B* cannot start until *t* network time units after the finish of Activity *A*. Most constraints are of this type, but *t* is usually zero.

(b) Start-to-start. Activity *B* cannot start until *t* network time units after the start of Activity *A*.

(c) Finish-to-finish. Activity *B* cannot be finished until *t* network time units after the finish of Activity *A*.

(d) Start-to-finish. Activity *B* cannot be finished until *t* network time units after the start of Activity *A*.

7.10 Activity constraint options in precedence networks

EARLY CONSIDERATION OF RESOURCE CONSTRAINTS

Nothing has been said so far about possible scarcity of resources and the additional constraints that such problems might impose on the network logic or estimated activity durations.

Consider, for example, the simplest case of a resource constraint, where one particular individual is going to have to perform several network activities single-handed. Assume that this person cannot perform two activities at the same time. The planner, knowing this, might be tempted to add links to the network to indicate this constraint and prevent any two of these activities from being planned as simultaneous tasks. But if all these activities lie on different paths in a complex network, where should these constraints be placed? Before time analysis the planner cannot know in which order all these jobs should be performed.

Similar worries about resources might attach to other activities where the resource requirements are more complex, when several activities can be allowed to run in parallel or overlap provided that the total resources needed do not exceed the total amount available.

Fortunately there is a simple solution to all these problems of resource constraints. At this stage in the planning, simply ignore them! The purpose of drawing the network is to establish the most desirable work pattern (assuming no resource constraints). Time analysis follows to establish the amount of float available, which effectively allots priority values to all activities. All of this information provides a sound basis for subsequent resource scheduling, which is a quite separate process (described in the next chapter).

Planning and scheduling have to be carried forward one step at a time, and consideration of resource constraints is a step that is not taken when the first network is drawn. However, the planner must use common sense in this respect. Suppose that an activity requiring skilled fitters has been estimated to require 150 man-hours, and that several people could work on the task if required (without getting in each other's way to any serious extent). The duration for this activity would therefore depend on the number of people assigned:

- 1 fitter for 20 days (20 man-days)
- 2 fitters for 10 days (20 man-days)
- 3 fitters for 8 days (24 man-days)
- 4 fitters for 7 days (28 man-days)
- and so on.

The correct approach for the planner is to ask the manager (or delegate) of the department responsible to say how many fitters would be best for this task, and write the corresponding duration on the network. The possible demands of other activities on these fitters are disregarded at this stage. However, if the company only employs two suitable fitters in total, the planner would be stupid to schedule more than two for this or any other activity. This is where common sense comes in. Notice that in this little example I have assumed that work efficiency reduces as more people as assigned to a single task, because they would tend to get in each other's way and impede progress.

8 *Scheduling Project Resources*

A small construction project is introduced in this chapter to illustrate network time analysis and resource scheduling. Resource scheduling can be a complex subject, but the most commonly used methods are described here.

RESOURCE SCHEDULING

Resource scheduling converts a project plan into a work schedule that takes account of the resources which can be made available. The schedule has to be practical. Workload peaks and troughs should be smoothed out as far as possible, whilst still attempting to finish the project at the earliest or required time.

In projects such as construction where much of the actual work is contracted out to others, resource scheduling becomes the responsibility of the subcontractors who employ the direct labour. That aspect of resource scheduling can be ignored here, except to mention that those subcontractors must be given reliable task dates by the project manager. If the project runs late the subcontractors' own schedules will be disrupted.

Most people think of resource scheduling in terms of people, but other resources (such as plant and machinery, bulk materials and cash) can be scheduled. The treatment of these non-labour resources is generally similar to manpower scheduling, except that the names and units of quantity will be different. Any commodity that can be quantified in linear units can be scheduled using the methods described here.

Physical working space is more difficult to schedule, particularly when complexities such as overhead clearance have to be considered. Those problems need solutions (usually involving computer graphics) which are not discussed here.

THE ROLE OF NETWORK ANALYSIS IN RESOURCE SCHEDULING

When a critical path network is drawn, attention has first to focus on the network logic and no considered account can be taken of the resources which will be available when work starts. A network cannot be used by itself to demonstrate the volume of resources needed at any given time. The start of each activity is assumed to be dependent only upon the completion of its preceding activities, and not on the availability of resources at the right time.

However, network time analysis will determine activity priorities in terms of their planned dates and float. Those results are a vital component of the subsequent resource scheduling process. Usually it is the activities with least remaining float that should get the highest priority and first claim for scarce resources. This is explained in the following project case example.

INTRODUCING THE GARAGE PROJECT

Project Definition

A small firm of builders has been commissioned to erect a detached garage. The building is to be constructed of brick, with a concrete floor, corrugated sheet roof, and with corrugated roof lights instead of windows. The wooden doors are to be made on site and hung on strap hinges. No heavy lifting is involved in this project and no activity needs more than two people. The planned start date is 13 May 2014 and completion is required as soon as possible.

Resources Available

The building firm engaged on the garage project is a very tiny outfit, comprising the not unusual father and son team. The father, no longer capable of sustained heavy work, is nevertheless a good all-round craftsman with long experience. The son, on the other hand, can best be described as a strong, willing lad, sound in wind and limb but lacking any special skill. This firm's resource availability can therefore be listed as follows:

Skilled persons: 1 (stated as 1S for the computer)
Labourers: 1 (stated as 1L for the computer).

If really stretched, this small company can call upon additional help, but it prefers to keep work in the family.

Task List and Cost Estimates

The task list for the garage project is shown in Figure 8.1. This lists all the principal tasks, together with their estimated materials costs. The activity ID codes refer to the network diagram, which is shown in Figure 8.2. Note that the activity boxes in this network do not conform to the standard set out in the previous chapter, in Figure 7.5. Although that standard is an ideal format, space limitation on the computer screen and on printouts prevents inclusion of all the data for each activity.

The estimated resource levels needed for each activity are written on the network diagram. For example, activity G016 has a duration of 2 days and needs one skilled person and one labourer, as indicated by the codes 2d 1S 1L. This means, in practice, one skilled person and one labourer working together full time for two days.

Activity ID	Activity description	Materials required	Cost of materials £
G001	Project start	No materials	
G002	Dig foundations	No materials	
G003	Make, prime door frame	Wood and primer	100
G004	Dig soakaway and trench	No materials	
G005	Make doors	Wood and sundries	300
G006	Cut roof timbers	Wood	400
G007	Concrete foundations	Concrete	200
G008	Position door frame	No materials	
G009	Lay underground pipe	Pipe and sundries	40
G010	Build main brick walls	Bricks and mortar	800
G011	Lay concrete floor	Concrete ingredients	200
G012	Prime the doors	Primer and sundries	20
G013	Fit RSJ lintel	Rolled steel joist (RSJ)	75
G014	Lay floor screed	Flooring compound	200
G015	Fit roof timbers	Fixings	20
G016	Case lintel, build parapets	Wood and concrete	70
G017	Fill drain trench	No materials	
G018	Fit fascia boards	Wood	50
G019	Fit roof sheets	Sheets and fixings	400
G020	Hang doors	Locks and hinges	100
G021	Fit gutters and pipes	Gutters, pipes, fixings	80
G022	Concrete over trench	Concrete ingredients	40
G023	Seal the roof	Sealant and sundries	50
G024	Paint all woodwork	Paint and sundries	40
G025	Project finish	No materials	

Resource code	Resource name	Resource cost £ per man-day
S	Skilled worker	200
L	Labourer	150

8.1 Garage project task list

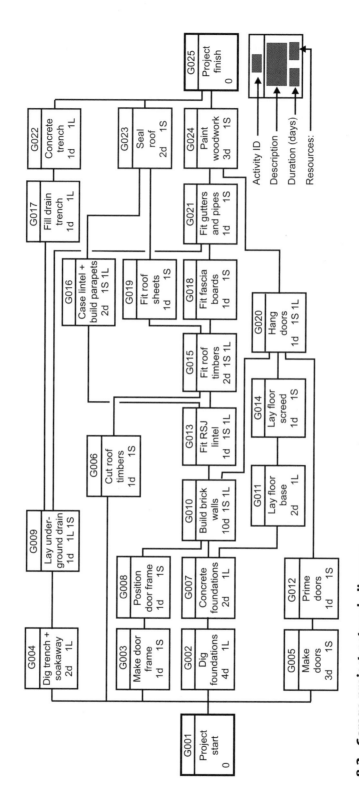

8.2 Garage project network diagram

The task list in Figure 8.1 also gives the daily cost rates for these resources. So the estimated total cost for activity G016 would be as follows:

1 skilled person for 2 days @ £200 per man-day:	£400
1 labourer for 2 days @ £150 per man-day:	£300
Materials:	£ 70
Total estimated cost of Activity G016	£770

The total estimated cost of all materials and labour for the garage will not be known until the computer has scheduled the resources and calculated all the activity costs.

Project Calendar

All scheduling for this garage project is to be based on a five-day working week. Saturdays and Sundays are not normally available for work. This is the default calendar assumed in most project management software. Although public holidays would have intervened in real life, they were ignored for this simple case study. In practice, all computer software will allow for public holidays to be removed from the working calendar, or for weekends to be worked.

GARAGE PROJECT NETWORK PLANNING

The Network Diagram

The network diagram in Figure 8.2 has deliberately been kept as simple as possible for clarity and to be able to print the schedules on these book pages. The plan assumes, for instance, that all necessary materials and machinery will be on site when needed. Also left out of this diagram is any provision for the time needed for concrete to cure.

Remember that a network diagram takes no account of any possible constraints caused by two or more activities competing for scarce resources. However, because this small firm has only one labourer and one skilled person, no activity has been estimated as needing more than this father and son family workforce.

Time Analysis

Figure 8.3 is the time analysis of the network diagram in Figure 8.2. That was calculated mentally, but for subsequent resource scheduling I used Primavera. It is a high-level, powerful and versatile program and, not surprisingly, it made short work of this tiny project. The activities in Figure 8.3 are listed in ascending order of their ID numbers.

Activity ID	Activity description	Duration (days)	Earliest start	Latest start	Earliest finish	Latest finish	Total float	Resources
G001	Project start	0	0	0	0	0	0	
G002	Dig foundations	4	0	0	4	4	0	1L
G003	Make, prime door frame	1	0	4	1	5	4	1S
G004	Dig soakaway/trench	2	0	17	2	19	17	1L
G005	Make doors	3	0	16	3	19	16	1S
G006	Cut roof timbers	1	0	16	1	17	16	1S
G007	Concrete foundations	2	4	4	6	6	0	1L
G008	Position door frame	1	1	5	2	6	4	1S
G009	Lay u/g drain pipe	1	2	19	3	20	17	1S 1L
G010	Build brick walls	10	6	6	16	16	0	1S 1L
G011	Lay floor base	2	6	17	8	19	11	1L
G012	Prime the doors	1	3	19	4	20	16	1S
G013	Fit RSJ lintel	1	16	16	17	17	0	1S 1L
G014	Lay floor screed	1	8	19	9	20	11	1S
G015	Fit roof timbers	2	17	17	19	19	0	1S 1L
G016	Case lintel, build ppts	2	17	20	19	22	3	1S 1L
G017	Fill drain trench	1	3	22	4	23	19	1L
G018	Fit fascia boards	1	19	19	20	20	0	1S
G019	Fit roof sheets	1	19	21	20	22	1	1S
G020	Hang doors	1	16	20	17	21	4	1S 1L
G021	Fit gutters and pipes	1	20	20	21	21	0	1S
G022	Concrete over trench	1	4	23	5	24	19	1L
G023	Seal the roof	2	20	22	22	24	2	1S
G024	Paint all woodwork	3	21	21	24	24	0	1S
G025	Project finish	0	24	24	24	24	0	

8.3 Garage project critical path network time analysis

Subsequent scheduling by Primavera converted all the day numbers of Figure 8.3 into calendar dates and revealed that if this project starts as planned on 13 May 2014, it should finish on 13 June 2014, provided that nothing goes terribly wrong and that there are adequate resources. But a big question mark hangs over those resources. Will the father and son team be enough to carry out all this work in the time available?

A FIRST LOOK AT THE GARAGE PROJECT RESOURCE SCHEDULE

The bar chart in Figure 8.4 is a conversion of the time analysis data given in Figure 8.3. Each bar is coded to show the type of resource needed, with solid black indicating one skilled person and each grey bar denoting the labourer.

All tasks have been placed at their earliest possible dates on the bar chart. A glance down some of the daily columns shows that there will be days when more than one person of each grade will be needed, unless the various jobs can be rearranged. It is obvious that some tasks must be deliberately delayed if the peak work overloads are to be smoothed out. But by how much can any task be delayed without affecting the project end date? That, of course, will depend on how much float each task has.

Before going on to examine float in a little more detail, one assumption has to be made. The customer for this garage wants it built as soon as possible. Meanwhile her shiny new car is having to stand out in the street, unprotected night and day. So, if the garage can be finished on 13 June 2014, that's when the customer wants it.

All float calculations for this project will therefore be based on trying to achieve the earliest possible completion date of 13 June 2014.

FLOAT

The network for the garage project (Figure 8.2) and its time analysis will be used here to illustrate how float is classified and calculated. Project day numbers are used here because the arithmetic is far easier than when calendar dates are used (a problem that vanishes when the computer is used).

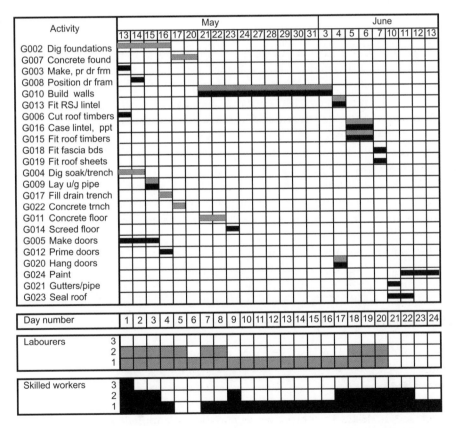

8.4   Garage project bar chart and histogram (resource aggregation)

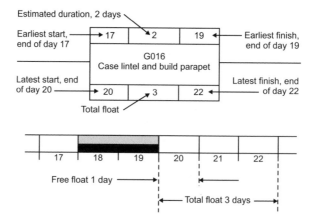

8.5 Garage project: float analysis of activity G016

Total Float

Consider activity G016, 'Case Lintel and build parapet'. For clarity, this activity is shown as a separate detail in Figure 8.5, which allows all the time analysis data to be included in the activity box. A glance at the network fragment shows that the earliest possible start for this activity is day 17 (which means the end of day 17 or the beginning of day 18). The latest permissible finish is the end of day 22. Allowing for the two-day duration of this activity, it is easy to see that its start (or finish) could be delayed by up to 3 days without causing delay to the activities that follow. This 3-day period is the total float possessed by the activity. That result is shown graphically in Figure 8.5.

Total float is defined as the amount by which an activity can be delayed if all its preceding activities take place at their earliest possible times and following activities are allowed to wait until their latest permissible times.

> Total float = latest permissible task finish time
> *minus*   the earliest possible task start time
> *minus*   the estimated task duration.

Applying the data from Figure 8.5 to this formula for activity G016:

> Total float = (22 = 17 − 2) = 3 days.

Free Float

If, because of delays in the project or through intentional resource scheduling, activity G016 takes place later than its earliest possible time, some (if not all) of its float will be eroded. This will usually have a knock-on effect through the network, robbing some of the float from activities which follow. In fact the float for any activity must always be seen in relation to how it is likely to affect, or be affected by, the float possessed by other activities in the network.

Consideration of these effects gives rise to definitions for two types of float in addition to total float. These are free float (described here) and independent float (which is sufficiently rare and unimportant to be ignored here).

Free float is defined as the amount of float available to a task or activity when all its preceding activities take place at their earliest possible times and the immediately following activity can still take place at its earliest possible time. This condition can only arise when an activity has more than one logical link at each end, and most activities will have zero free float. However, activity G016 does have one day of free float. This is calculated as follows:

Free float = earliest start date of the activity (or activities) immediately following *minus* the earliest finish of the activity under consideration.

From the network diagram in Figure 8.2, it can be seen that the activity immediately following G016 is G023. The time analysis in Figure 8.3 shows the earliest start of activity G023 to be day 20. Applying the above formula to find the free float of activity G016 gives:

Free float = (20 – 19) which is one day.

Do not be dismayed by the apparent complexity of these calculations, especially when calendar dates are substituted for day numbers. It will all come right easily when the problem is put to the computer.

Remaining Float

The float possessed by any activity is at risk of erosion from the moment when project resource scheduling starts right up to the time when the activity is completed. Total float can be reduced, for example, as a result of a conscious decision to delay the planned start of an activity in the resource scheduling process (to obtain a smoother workload pattern). There is also the risk that preceding activities will run late, absorbing some or all of the float.

For practical purposes, once a project is started the project manager is not interested in the total float that an activity had in the beginning, when the network was first drawn. It is the residue of the total float still possessed by each uncompleted activity that should concern the project manager. This is the *remaining float*. Many computer programs do not report remaining float. However, the total float reported by the computer after rescheduling in line with progress achievement should be the remaining float.

Activities with Negative Float

Suppose that the critical path through a network has a total estimated duration of 100 weeks. The end activity will therefore have an earliest possible completion time of 100. Barring other considerations, the latest permissible completion time for the project will be at the end of the 100th week. Time analysis will, in the usual way, produce one or more critical paths back through to the start of the network in which all the critical activities have zero total float.

Suppose, however, that those 'other considerations' include a promise to the customer that the project will be completed in 90 weeks. The latest permissible project end date is therefore 10 weeks before its earliest possible date. All activities that were previously on the critical path with zero total float will now have a total float of minus 10 weeks.

Negative float can be caused whenever fixed target dates are imposed on the end activity (or on any other activity in a project network) that are impossible to meet. The cause may be a critical path that is longer than the time allowed by the target date. Negative float can also occur as a result of imposing resource restrictions during scheduling, so that there are insufficient resources to carry out all the tasks in the time allowed by the critical path. That happened in the resource-limited schedule shown in Figure 8.8, which will be explained later.

GARAGE PROJECT RESOURCE SCHEDULING

Resource scheduling was carried out both mentally and using a computer for the examples in this chapter. The mental solutions were only possible because of the very small size of this project.

Before project managers had access to computers, all scheduling had to be done manually and the most convenient method used chart boards. Bar charts could be set up so that the tasks could be moved back and forwards until a smooth workload was achieved. Various proprietary mechanical chart designs made this possible, by using horizontal slots, magnetic strips or (commonly) pegboard with the holes set on a 6mm grid. Of course, making the adjustments to remove work peaks whilst observing all the dependencies between activities was quite an art and sometimes tedious.

The histogram at the foot of Figure 8.4 showed the unacceptable resource usage patterns that resulted from trying to schedule all activities at their earliest possible times. However, with the knowledge of how much float each activity has, some intelligent delaying of non-critical tasks can smooth the resource usage patterns. The three basic options are shown in Figure 8.6.

The histograms in Figure 8.6 were calculated by hand and repeated, somewhat less perfectly, using a number of different computer programs. However, for the current argument it does not matter how these charts were produced. They are presented here to demonstrate three different options in resource scheduling.

Resource Aggregation

Look first at the top pair of histograms shown in Figure 8.6. These are repeated from those shown at the foot of the bar chart in Figure 8.4. They show the numbers of each resource type that would be needed on each weekday to perform all the garage project activities on their earliest possible dates. The numbers of skilled people needed each day to complete this project were found by adding the number of times that a black bar appeared in each daily column. Repeating the process for the grey bars gave the daily numbers of unskilled labourers needed.

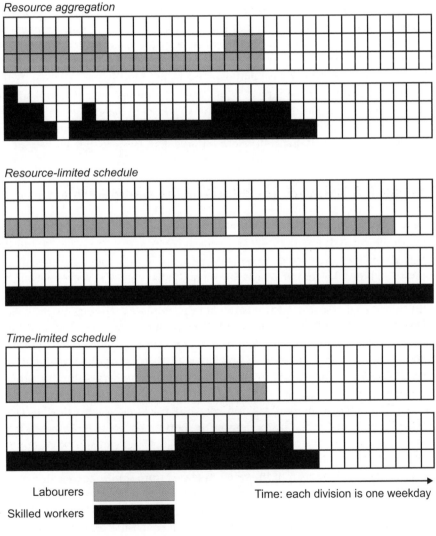

8.6 Three different resource usage patterns for the garage project

If resources were available in ample supply, then perhaps this schedule could be accepted. However, we know that the garage team has only one skilled and one unskilled person available, so would be unable to provide the extra people needed without calling in help from outside. But any schedule that has peak workloads interspersed with idle periods is inefficient and inconvenient because it implies either that people will be overworked on some days and idle on others, or that impossible hiring and firing of workpeople will be needed.

Resource Limited Schedule

Suppose now that the garage builder has decided that on no account will he hire any additional help, so that he and his unskilled son will have to do all the work.

A plan made to satisfy this requirement is known as a resource-limited schedule. Some activities are moved to later dates to remove the overloads. Activities with float are moved first but, if absolutely necessary, some critical activities might have to be moved and then the project end date will be delayed.

The result for the garage project is shown in the middle pair of histograms in Figure 8.6. The very smooth, optimized result shown here was calculated mentally. I also ran this calculation using several different computer programs and they generally produced the same result. The project end-date was put back from 13 June to 26 June 2014, as shown later in Figure 8.8.

Time-limited Resource Levelling for the Garage Project

Unfortunately for the master builder of the garage project, the customer is vociferous and short-tempered. Her raised voice has attracted quite a doorstep audience and she has left the builder and everyone else within earshot in no doubt that she will not wait until 26 June 2014 for her garage. She insists on having her new car safely under cover by the evening of 13 June. The schedule must, therefore, be recalculated.

In this revised case, the answer is to plan to complete the garage by its earliest possible time analysis date, take on additional resources as required, but adjust the timings of individual activities *within their float* to remove the workload peaks as far as possible. The latest times from network analysis must be observed for all the critical tasks. These times could be shown only as day numbers before the project start date was known (Figure 8.3) but computer scheduling from the given start date will convert all these unhelpful day numbers into more practicable calendar dates.

The pair of time-limited histograms at the bottom of Figure 8.6 resulted from rescheduling the garage project manually. Now the project can still be completed by 13 June 2014. It is true that extra resources are needed, but these are fewer and used far more smoothly than in the result obtained from simple aggregation.

Extra resource availability can sometimes be provided simply by asking people to work longer hours. However, projects should not be scheduled with the intention of using overtime. As work on a project proceeds, overtime becomes a valuable reserve resource, to be called upon only in emergencies, when critical activities are in danger of running late. Overtime should normally be held in reserve against such contingencies, and the stated resource availability levels should be limited to the numbers employed during normal working hours.

COMPUTER SCHEDULING OF THE GARAGE AND OTHER PROJECTS

It is no longer necessary to detail the many advantages that the use of a computer can bring, both for processing data and for communicating it to others within and outside the organization.

Resource-limited Versus Time-limited Scheduling

All competent software will give the project manager the option of choosing between time-limited and resource-limited scheduling.

Figure 8.7 is an analogy of how that choice can affect the scheduled times. In Figure 8.7 you are asked to imagine the project as a balloon filled with an incompressible liquid. This volume of liquid represents the total amount of project work needed. Try to squeeze the project into the time allowed in a time-limited calculation, and the balloon will extend upwards beyond the available resources limit. Alternatively, squeeze the balloon flat until it lies within the available resources, and the project will spill over into extra time.

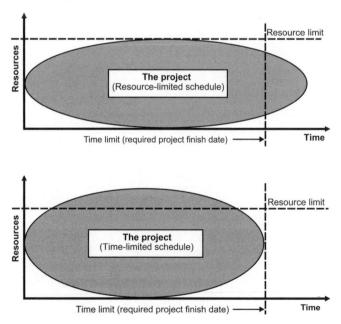

8.7   Time-limited versus resource-limited priority rules

Figure 8.8 displays the resource-limited schedule for the garage project. The data were obtained using Primavera, which is one of the few project management software suites that have a long pedigree and truly deserve the adjectives 'powerful' and 'versatile' (Open Plan, Artemis, Micro Planner X-Pert and 4c Systems are others).

Figure 8.8 is effectively a 'work-to' list for the project. Primavera, in common with Microsoft Project and other software, can display this tabulation at the left-hand side of a screen that also contains a bar chart. Additional columns can be selected from drop-down menus to include many different quantities, including free float, actual cost, budgeted cost, and so on. However, the more columns that are added, the more difficult it becomes to display the bar chart on a readable scale.

Task ID	Task description	Dur (days)	Earliest start	Earliest finish	Latest start	Latest finish	Total float
G001	Project start	0	13MAY14	13MAY14	13MAY14	13MAY14	0
G003	Make, prime dr frame	1	13MAY14	13MAY14	17MAY14	17MAY14	4
G002	Dig foundations	4	13MAY14	16MAY14	13MAY14	16MAY14	0
G008	Position door frame	1	14MAY14	14MAY14	20MAY14	20MAY14	4
G005	Make doors	3	15MAY14	17MAY14	04JUN14	06JUN14	14
G007	Concrete foundations	2	17MAY14	20MAY14	17MAY14	20MAY14	0
G006	Cut roof timbers	1	20MAY14	20MAY14	04JUN14	04JUN14	11
G010	Build brick walls	10	21MAY14	03JUN14	21MAY14	03JUN14	0
G013	Fit RSJ lintel	1	04JUN14	04JUN14	04JUN14	04JUN14	0
G015	Fit roof timbers	2	05JUN14	06JUN14	05JUN14	06JUN14	0
G018	Fit fascia boards	1	07JUN14	07JUN14	07JUN14	07JUN14	0
G011	Lay concrete base	2	07JUN14	10JUN14	05JUN14	06JUN14	-2
G012	Prime doors	1	10JUN14	10JUN14	07JUN14	07JUN14	-1
G014	Lay floor screed	1	11JUN14	11JUN14	07JUN14	07JUN14	-2
G004	Dig soakaway/trench	2	11JUN14	12JUN14	05JUN14	06JUN14	-4
G019	Fit roof sheets	1	12JUN14	12JUN14	11JUN14	11JUN14	-1
G009	Lay underground pipe	1	13JUN14	13JUN14	07JUN14	07JUN14	-4
G017	Fill drain trench	1	14JUN14	14JUN14	12JUN14	12JUN14	-2
G021	Fit gutters and pipes	1	14JUN14	14JUN14	10JUN14	10JUN14	-4
G016	Case lintel, build ppts	2	17JUN14	18JUN14	10JUN14	11JUN14	-5
G020	Hang doors	1	19JUN14	19JUN14	10JUN14	10JUN14	-7
G022	Concrete drain trench	1	20JUN14	20JUN14	13JUN14	13JUN14	-5
G024	Paint all woodwork	3	20JUN14	24JUN14	11JUN14	13JUN14	-7
G023	Seal roof	2	25JUN14	26JUN14	12JUN14	13JUN14	-9
G025	Project finish	0	26JUN14	26JUN14	13JUN14	13JUN14	-9

8.8 Garage project resource-limited schedule (data from Primavera)

The resource-limited schedule in Figure 8.8 shows that the earliest possible dates are, in many cases, later than the latest permissible dates because of the resource-limited scheduling. As a result, negative float has been generated (and faithfully reported by Primavera).

Graphics and Other Computer Reports

Project management software can display and print network diagrams, bar charts, resource histograms and all manner of other graphical displays, improved visually by the use of colour. Cost control data can be linked to the schedules, allowing budget cost curves, cost tables, and other presentations of planned and recorded expenditure to be printed.

For example, Figure 8.9 is a cost/time graph for the garage project, based on a report produced by Primavera after resource-limited scheduling. The height of each vertical bar is scaled according to the labour and material costs of the tasks scheduled for each working day. Notice that no costs are scheduled for weekend days. The curve running above the bars is the cumulative estimated project cost, which culminates in the total project cost estimate at the right-hand side.

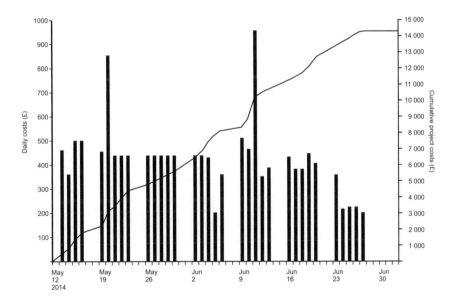

8.9   Garage project cost and time graphs, with resource-limited scheduling

I derived Figure 8.10 from data produced by Microsoft Project. This shows the day-by-day expected resource usage and cumulative project costs of the garage project, again running with the resource limited rule. If all the projects in an organization can be scheduled together by the computer, reports such as this are a valuable input to company manpower planning and recruitment. They can also indicate falling workloads, often revealing the need to look for new work.

GARAGE PROJECT SCHEDULED RESOURCE USAGE AND COST

Date	Resource L: Labourer				Resource S: Skilled				Task matls cost £	Cum. cost £
	Avail.	Used	Not used	Cost £	Avail	Used	Not used	Cost £		
13 May 14	1	1	-	150		1	-	200	100	450
14 May 14	1	1	-	150	1	1	-	200	-	800
15 May 14	1	1	-	150	1	1	-	200	150	1300
16 May 14	1	1	-	150	1	1	-	200	150	1800
19 May 14	1	1	-	150	1	1	-	200	100	2250
20 May 14	1	1	-	150	1	1	-	200	500	3100
21 May 14	1	1	-	150	1	1	-	200	80	3530
22 May 14	1	1	-	150	1	1	-	200	80	3960
23 May 14	1	1	-	150	1	1	-	200	80	4390
26 May 14	1	1	-	150	1	1	-	200	80	4820
27 May 14	1	1	-	150	1	1	-	200	80	5250
28 May 14	1	1	-	150	1	1	-	200	80	5680
29 May 14	1	1	-	150	1	1	-	200	80	6110
30 May 14	1	1	-	150	1	1	-	200	80	6540
02 Jun 14	1	1	-	150	1	1	-	200	80	6970
03 Jun 14	1	1	-	150	1	1	-	200	80	7400
04 Jun 14	1	1	-	150	1	1	-	200	75	7825
05 Jun 14	1	-	1	-	1	1	-	200	-	8025
06 Jun 14	1	1	-	150	1	1	-	200	10	8385
09 Jun 14	1	1	-	150	1	1	-	200	160	8895
10 Jun 14	1	1	-	150	1	1	-	200	120	9365
11 Jun 14	1	1	-	150	1	1	-	200	600	10315
12 Jun 14	1	1	-	150	1	1	-	200	-	10665
13 Jun 14	1	1	-	150	1	1	-	200	40	11055
16 Jun 14	1	1	-	150	1	1	-	200	80	11485
17 Jun 14	1	1	-	150	1	1	-	200	35	11870
18 Jun 14	1	1	-	150	1	1	-	200	35	12255
19 Jun 14	1	1	-	150	1	1	-	200	100	12705
20 Jun 14	1	1	-	150	1	1	-	200	54	13109
23 Jun 14	1	1	-	150	1	1	-	200	13	13472
24 Jun 14	1	-	1	-	1	1	-	200	13	13685
25 Jun 14	1	-	1	-	1	1	-	200	25	13910
26 Jun 14	1	-	1	-	1	1	-	200	25	14135
27 Jun 14	1	-	1	-	1	1	-	200	-	14335
30 Jun 14	1	-	1	-	1	-	1	-	-	14355
01 Jul 14	1	-	1	-	1	-	1	-	-	14355
02 Jul 14	1	-	1	-	1	-	1	-	-	14355
03 Jul 14	1	-	1	-	1	-	1	-	-	14355
04 Jul 14	1	-	1	-	1	-	1	-	-	14355
05 Jul 14		-	1	-	1	-	1	-	-	14355

8.10   Garage project resource usage forecast

Although graphical displays will sometimes impress senior executives and others who are unskilled in the arts of project management, tables in spreadsheet form are better in providing accurate data because the times and amounts can be read off immediately without having to read them off a scale.

Network Plots

A network plot is particularly useful early in the data processing proceedings and at every update of the plan. The plot will show whether or all the data describing the activities and their connecting links have been correctly keyed into the system.

Computer programs vary considerably in their ability to plot networks sensibly. Poor examples will be difficult to interpret visually, with some links going from right to left, showing avoidable crossovers, and sometimes even with two or more links running along the same line so that they become mixed. Early versions of one program even plotted one activity on top of another, so that a 150-activity network would look like a 120-activity plan. Primavera, Open Plan, 4c and Microsoft Project were tried for the garage project, and all gave good results.

Network plots tend to spread over large areas of paper. A planner with only an A4 printer will find that many sheets will be needed, all of which have to be cut and pasted together before a complete network can be seen. For this reason, I have not attempted to illustrate any results here. A digital printer that can plot on large sheets or wide rolls or paper is a necessity for companies.

Filtering

After a big network has been processed, a large volume of data is stored in the computer. If all possible reports were to be produced, the result might be an unmanageable pile of paper, impressive for its bulk, but not for much else. It follows that the project manager must manage the data carefully, ensuring that reports are concise, well-presented and as effective as possible for their intended purpose.

The data content of every report must be carefully considered, to ensure that each recipient gets information that is particularly useful or relevant to them (preferably on a 'needs-to-know' basis). This is achieved by the filtering (editing), made possible by giving each activity record a departmental report code that will identify the manager or supervisor who is primarily responsible for carrying out the task. Other ways of filtering include reporting on selected resources, or by choosing only activities that have been designated as milestones. Most programs provide a menu from which filtering options can be selected.

All unwanted data should be excluded from reports. For example, the planner might choose to filter out all activities that have already been completed. Senior managers might need to see only milestone reports.

Sorting

Another important aspect of reports is the sequence in which data are presented. The process of sorting achieves the best sequence for any particular purpose. For example, a departmental manager or supervisor responsible for issuing work needs a report that lists jobs in order of their earliest or scheduled start dates. A progress clerk or expediter sometimes needs a report that lists jobs or materials deliveries in order of their expected delivery dates.

Work-to Lists

A tabulation of all activities sorted in ascending order of their scheduled start dates is the prime tool for issuing work. If such reports can be produced after resource levelling and then filtered to suit each manager on the project, every recipient of their work-to list can feel confident because of the following:

- Every job has been sequenced by network analysis so that it should not be scheduled to start before it is logically feasible.
- The rate of working expected from each department or, in other words, the number of activities shown as starting in each period, has been determined by resource scheduling, so that every task listed should be achievable with the available resources.

Figure 8.8 is the resource-limited work-to list for the garage project produced by Primavera. The columns headed 'Early start' and 'Early finish' give the recommended (scheduled) working dates. The 'latest' dates are for information only, being the latest dates needed to finish the project by 13 June (impossible by the computer in this case owing to the limited resources available).

Executive Summary Reports

Most programs make provision for one-page project summary reports, intended as management overviews. If more than one project is contained in the system, some programs will allow summary reports to be printed out concisely for all these projects in a type of report sometimes known as a project directory. Some programs can produce imaginative graphics for this purpose, for example including RAG reporting in which **r**ed, **a**mber or **g**reen signals are placed in traffic signal style against each item to show respectively whether it is running over time or budget, is at risk, or is on plan.

RECAPITULATION

Now we are about two-thirds of the way through this book, but we have not yet progressed along the project life cycle beyond the planning stages. No actual work authorization or progressing has yet been discussed. The attention given here to all these planning processes signals the importance of defining, planning and organizing the project as well as possible before embarking upon actual work or serious expenditure.

In addition to an initial financial business case (or business plan), the outcome of all these preliminary processes should be detailed work-to lists based on critical path planning. Where direct labour is to be employed, resource scheduling will be needed to make these work-to lists achievable.

Many project management processes depend on logical thought. Making sense of the myriad of problems and pressures that face any project organization can seem to be an insurmountable problem because there are simply too many variables. But in mathematics the way of dealing with a large number of unknown variables is to solve them one at a time. So it is in project planning. Figure 8.11 identifies seven logical steps that can solve most of the variables and lead to a practicable plan of work.

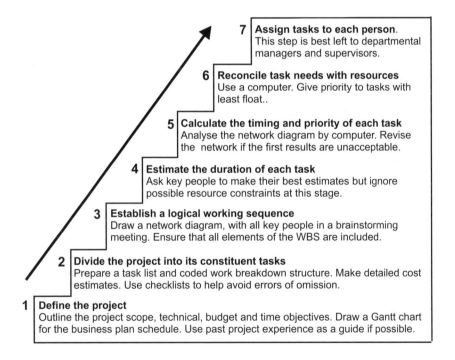

8.11 Seven logical steps to a practical project resource schedule

9 *Implementing the Project Plan*

Once authorization has been received, the project ceases to be merely an object for planning and speculation and becomes instead a live entity, to which the contractor is fully committed. To achieve all the project objectives, the appropriate project organization has to be in place. All participants must be made aware of the particular role they will be expected to play.

A common risk to projects is failure to start work on time. Very long delays can be caused by prevarication, legal or planning difficulties, shortage of information, lack of funds or other resources, and a host of other reasons. All of these factors can place a project manager in a difficult or impossible position, because *if a project is not allowed to start on time it can hardly be expected to finish on time.*

PROJECT AUTHORIZATION

Project authorization by the customer or project owner means giving formal written instruction authorizing the contractor to proceed with the project on terms that have previously been negotiated and agreed. For in-house management projects, remember that the 'customer' is the company itself and the 'contractor' is the internal division or department responsible.

Initial Registration and Numbering

Every new project should be formally 'entered into the system' so that all the necessary accounting, planning, progressing and other administrative procedures can be put in place.

One of the first steps is to add the new project to the project register and allocate a project number. This number should preferably be built in subsequently as an identifying component to drawing and equipment specification numbers, cost codes, timesheets and other important project documents.

Whenever it is necessary to retrieve information about a project, current or long past, the project register (or its archived information) is usually the best starting place. In most management information systems and archives the project number is the essential element leading to the various document files and project data. However, a well-kept register should also allow a search on keywords, such as the project manager's name, the customer's name, project title, and so forth.

Internal Project Authorization Document and Work Instructions

Although a few companies have a laissez-faire approach to project authorization, it is usually agreed that a formal document should be issued to approve expenditure on every new project. Project authorizations come in many designs and, depending on the type of project, might be named Works Order, Project Charter, or some other possibility. An example of a project authorization document based on some projects in my past experience is given in Figure 9.1.

Ideally the authorizing document should outline departmental and purchasing cost budgets, give planned start and finish dates, details of the customer's order, pricing information, invoicing and delivery instructions, and so on. An essential item on a project authorization is the signature of a member of the contractor's senior management to signal that the project is authorized and that work (and therefore expenditure) can begin.

Project authorizations are usually distributed to all company departments (not necessarily as hard copy). The project manager should also receive all supporting technical and commercial documents (initial sketches and drawings, specifications, schedules and so forth).

PRELIMINARY ORGANIZATION OF THE PROJECT

Even when a clear technical specification has been prepared there are often many loose ends to be tied up before actual work can start. The extent and nature of these preliminary activities naturally depend on the type and size of project.

When the project manager has been named, an organization chart should be drawn and published to show all key people or agencies concerned with the project. It must include senior members of all external groups who are to have any responsibility in the project. If the organization is very large, the usual arrangement is to produce an overall summary chart and then draw a series of smaller charts which allow some of the groups to be shown in more detail.

Responsibility Matrix

People must know what is expected of them. One tool which can assist the project manager to allocate responsibilities is the linear responsibility matrix, an example of which is shown in Figure 9.2. The job titles of key members of the organization are listed above the matrix columns and important task categories are listed along

PROJECT AUTHORIZATION

Client _____

Scope of work _____
_____
_____
_____
_____

Source documents _____
_____
_____

Project number (to be entered by accounts department) ☐☐☐☐☐☐

Project title ☐☐☐☐☐☐☐☐☐☐☐☐☐☐☐☐☐☐

Project manager (name) _____ Staff number ☐☐☐☐

Project engineer (name) _____ Staff number ☐☐☐☐

Project start date (enter as 01-JAN-14) ☐☐-☐☐☐-☐☐

Target finish date (enter as 01-JAN-14) ☐☐-☐☐☐-☐☐

Contract type:
Reimbursable ☐   Lump sum ☐   Other (Specify) _____

Estimate of man-hours

Standard cost grade	1	2	3	4	5	6	7	8
Man-hour totals								

Notes:

....
Authorization (1)   *Authorization (2)*

Project manager	Marketing	Contracts dept.	Purchasing		
Project engineer	Central registry	Cost/planning	Accounts dept.		

9.1   A project authorization form used by a mining engineering company

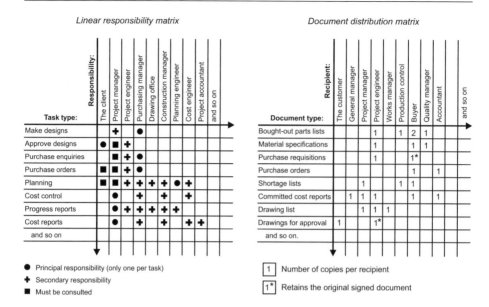

Linear responsibility matrix

Document distribution matrix

● Principal responsibility (only one per task)
+ Secondary responsibility
■ Must be consulted

1 Number of copies per recipient

1* Retains the original signed document

9.2 Two useful matrix charts

the rows. Symbols placed at the appropriate matrix intersections show primary and secondary responsibility for each listed task category.

Distribution of Correspondence and Other Paper Documents

The contractor will be well advised to take control procedures for project correspondence seriously. The contractor could easily find itself in a difficult position if it were to lose vital letters or other documents. Positive steps must be taken to deal with the routing and control of documented information across all external parts of the project organization.

In large projects it is good practice for each different company involved to nominate a person to act as a control point for receiving and sending all formal written communications and technical documents. Each nominated addressee is made responsible for seeing that the documents or the information contained in them is made known to all the relevant people within their own organization. Of course this procedure can apply only to documents that have legal or technical significance, and not to the hundreds of informal communications such as casual e-mails.

It is necessary to consider and list the types of documents that will be generated throughout the life of the project, and then decide who needs to receive copies as a matter of routine. This should usually be on a 'needs to know' rather than 'wants to know' basis (except that all requests for documents from the customer must be looked upon favourably unless these would give away information that the contractor wishes to remain confidential).

If the documents are to be made available over a network, it might be necessary to impose different levels of access for security purposes, thus preventing unauthorized people from seeing sensitive or confidential data.

Once the regular distribution or availability of documents has been agreed, the decision can be depicted on a matrix chart, arranged in similar fashion to the responsibility matrix already described. One of these is shown in the right-hand section of Figure 9.2. The names of the authorized recipients are placed at the tops of vertical columns and various documents under consideration are listed down the left-hand side. Use of this chart is self-explanatory.

Design Standards and Procedures

The contractor will have to investigate whether or not the project calls for any special design standards, safety requirements, or compliance with statutory regulations. These issues usually have cost implications, so that all or most of these requirements should have been established earlier, at the project definition stage.

Drawings made for a project sometimes become the property of the customer, who will expect to be given a file of all the original drawings at the end of the project (the contractor would, of course, retain a complete copy).

The contractor might be asked to use the customer's own drawing numbering system. Usual practice in such cases is to number each drawing twice, using the customer's system and the contractor's normal standard. These dual numbers must be cross-referenced, but that is simple with the drawings register filed in a computer.

Choice of Project Planning and Control Procedures

Companies that regularly carry out projects may have at their disposal a considerable range of planning and control procedures. At the start of each new project these can be reviewed to determine which should be used. Factors affecting this choice are the size and complexity of the project, the degree of difficulty and risk expected in meeting the end objectives, the number and locations of outside organizations and the wishes or directions of the customer.

Project Handbook

For large projects contractors will compile a project handbook (also known as a project procedures manual). This lists the procedures that will apply to the particular project. It will include such things as the names of key personnel, organization charts, responsibility matrix, document distribution matrix, and the names and addresses of all key organizations with their relevant incoming and outgoing correspondence contact points. A short version, containing only matters pertaining to correspondence, can be issued as a secretaries' manual.

PHYSICAL PREPARATIONS AND ORGANIZATION

It is obvious that physical preparations must be made for any project that requires accommodation, plant, equipment, services such as gas, electric power, compressed air, water and so on. It is equally obvious that there is no typical case, because the requirements of every project depend very much on the nature of the project and the practices of its contractor. At one end of the scale is the project that will simply follow another in a factory or office, using the same staff, management and facilities. At the opposite extreme is the international project involving several large companies and a construction site in the middle of a desert with no communicating rail or road and no other existing infrastructure. In the latter case, making physical preparation for the main project is, in itself, a collection of very large subprojects. Any discussion of physical preparations in this chapter must, therefore, be in general terms.

Checklists

All project managers will know the frustration caused during the initial days and weeks when, keen to start and with deadlines to meet, work cannot start because there is no information, no staff and a general lack of other facilities.

Lack of information is often the worst of these problems. This may not be about the main objectives and features of the intended project but is more likely to be about the hundred-and-one annoying details which have to be resolved before work can start.

The value of checklists is mentioned in several places in this book, and no apology is needed or made for giving additional space to this subject here. Standard checklists, applicable to all projects, present and future, can be used as questionnaires to pre-empt information requirements. The best checklists are developed and refined through experience, so that lessons learned on each project are remembered and put to use on projects that follow.

Construction site checklist example

An example where a checklist is particularly useful is when a construction site organization has to be established, especially when this is to be overseas. Even for an experienced organization, that can be an enormous operation. All sorts of questions have to be asked, and answered. Some questions should already have been answered when the proposal was researched (see Figure 2.2, for example). When the project becomes real, these questions and answers have a more definite and detailed aspect, as shown in the checklist fragment in Figure 9.3. It is clearly important to get these answers as soon as possible.

How many people will be working on site?
How many of these people will be:
-   our own permanent staff?
-   our own fixed-term contract staff, hired for this project only?
-   local recruits? (will they need training?)
-   client's staff?
-   subcontractors' staff?
What accommodation must be provided?
-   how much?
-   what standard?
-   who will provide it?
-   rent free?
What are the local immigration rules?
-   passports and visas?
-   work permits?
-   any racial prejudices?
Local employment laws and practices?
What about expatriates' wives and families?
Standard terms of employment?
Pay and personal taxation?
Insurances:
-   staff related?
-   work related?
Staff medical, welfare and leisure facilities?
Climate?
Site access:
-   road?
-   rail?
-   air?
-   other?
Vehicle fleet:
-   personnel carriers?
-   goods and heavy materials?
-   how provided?
-   how managed and maintained?
Construction plant:
-   what is needed?
-   when?
-   how provided?
-   how maintained?

9.3   Fragment of a checklist for an overseas construction site

GETTING WORK STARTED

Kick-off Meeting

When the newly appointed project manager has collected his or her wits and absorbed the contents of the project specification (which will probably entail some late nights), the most urgent job is to mobilize all the project resources and tell the key participants what is expected of them.

This process takes place in different stages and by a variety of methods. The first executive action of the project manager is usually to call an initial meeting, often called the 'kick-off'meeting, which gives the project manager the opportunity to outline the main features of the project to managers whose departments will work on the project, and to the most senior design staff and other key people. A good idea is to invite a member of the company's senior management to introduce the new project and its project manager.

If the project is organized as a team, the project manager will have the advantage of talking to people who are going to be directly responsible to him or her. If the organization is a functional matrix, the task is more difficult – even getting people to attend the meeting becomes a question more of invitation or persuasion rather than a direct summons.

Whatever the circumstances, the skilled project manager will make the best possible use of the kick-off meeting to get the project off to a good start. Everyone should leave the meeting with a clear picture of the project's objectives, the part that they are expected to play in achieving them, and a sense of keenness and motivation to get on with the job.

Initial Planning Information

It is unlikely that early plans will exist in sufficient detail for issuing and controlling work on mainstream activities, but two aspects of initial plans have to be mentioned:

1. First project schedules are often only a simple summary of major tasks, with no idea at that stage of how the project will be broken down later into detailed, day-to-day tasks. Yet those early plans will probably have been used in a project proposal or business case and thus will have set the promised overall project time frame. In other words, when the project is authorized, the calculation of detailed plans will have the objective of meeting a project completion date that has already been promised.
2. The absence of very detailed plans at the start often does not matter, because the very first project tasks are either administrative or to review and finalize design concepts.

Two sets of initial plans should, therefore, be available for issue at the start. These are:

1. A summary plan giving committed dates for the whole project. This should accompany the project authorization document. It might be a bar chart but at this early stage it might just be a list of target dates or project milestones.
2. A checklist and plan for preliminary activities. Every contractor learns the preliminary activities needed to set up a new project and establish its procedures and design standards. One company in my experience designed a checklist in the form of a standard network diagram for use at the start of every project. Time estimates were not used on this network. Its value was as a checklist of preliminary activities in their logical sequence.

Of course detailed plans and work schedules must be made for the project as soon as practicable after project authorization. Early plans will often show very late delivery dates, and these will have to be worked and reworked until a schedule results that will satisfy the delivery promises already made to the customer, or given in a business case.

DETAILED PLANS AND WORK INSTRUCTIONS

Importance of Personal Agreement and Commitment

Earlier chapters described methods for planning and scheduling. At least one senior representative from every key project function should have some share in formulating (or at least agreeing) each detailed plan because no plan can be imposed successfully in isolation. A schedule of tasks must have the acceptance and support of all managers and supervisors who will subsequently be bound by its content and timing.

Issuing Work Schedules: Targeting Instructions for Action

As soon as the first detailed plans and resource schedules are available, the computer can produce a work-to list that is specific to every project department, showing only those tasks for which each departmental manager is responsible. This is achieved by filtering computer reports, using departmental codes allocated to tasks.

Instructions are often ignored when they are issued to too many people, instead of being targeted to the person responsible for action. There are two potential risks if a task instruction is put in a document that goes to several departmental managers:

1. Each manager may do nothing and rely on the others to carry out the instruction, in which case no one might take action and the job will not get done;
2. One task could be performed in two or more places, duplicating the work. This can be a risk in projects where orders for equipment and materials are placed from more than one purchasing department (which can happen in international projects).

Carefully filtered work-to lists have the advantage of being specific to their addressees, so that management responsibility for every item on each list is the clear responsibility of the recipient.

Work-to-lists need only be provided in detail to cover a few weeks ahead; longer term summaries should be provided to help departmental managers to recruit or reserve the necessary people. All of this is readily achievable with the filtering and sorting capabilities of competent project management software. However, that software has to be chosen with care.

Work-to Lists and the Authority of Departmental Managers

The instructions or reminders contained in work-to lists should in no way detract from the personal authority vested in each departmental manager.

Although the source of these schedules is likely to be the project management office (PMO), the data in them should derive from the detailed project plans that were originally reviewed and agreed by departmental managers. The authority of those managers, far from being undermined, is reinforced.

Each manager receives a timed list of the work required of their department but, within that time frame, is free to allocate the work to individuals within the department and to direct and control it (the last of the seven steps described at the end of the previous chapter). With work-to lists resulting from sensible resource scheduling, there should be no chronic overloads, although temporary overloads are always a risk.

Work-to Lists in Relation to Departmental Work Procedures

Work-to-lists can be regarded as departmental orders or as planning reminders, depending on the department to which they are sent.

Work-to lists for design engineering

In engineering design departments, the work-to lists will contain some tasks that can be allocated to individuals with no need to plan in any greater detail. However, project schedules are not always produced with sufficient detail for the day-to-day allocation of all work. It might still be necessary for managers and supervisors to make subplans, breaking tasks down further into smaller parts and planning how these will be allocated to individuals.

For instance, a network activity usually summarizes a group of drawings needed for a small work package or subassembly, and it is not usually desirable or possible to have a separate network activity for every individual project drawing or for every small item to be purchased. Drawing lists or drawing schedules, and purchase control schedules, bills of materials or material take-offs are needed to show a greater level of detail than is possible in the network diagram and its associated work-to lists. Thus design managers and their staff will have to carry out some planning in fine detail themselves.

The inclusion of estimated costs and target dates on work-to lists can help to make highly trained technologists aware that they have time and cost responsibilities – in addition to the creative aspects of their work that they enjoy most.

Work-to lists for production departments in manufacturing projects

Work-to lists for manufacturing would usually be sent to the production manager or production controller, who would continue to issue works orders, job tickets, route cards and other documents customarily used throughout the manufacturing organization.

The levels of detail shown in project networks (and, therefore, in their resulting work-to lists) are bound to be far coarser than those needed for the day-to-day planning and control of factory operations. For example, work-to lists can provide the scheduled start and required finish dates for each assembly and subassembly but they will not specify a greater degree of work breakdown.

Thus the manufacturing organization will use its own production engineering, planning and control facilities to interpret drawings, identify the parts and materials required and carry out detailed production scheduling. This must be done to satisfy the dates scheduled on the work-to lists but, when project resource scheduling has been used, the overall rate of working requested by the project manager should lie within the capacity of the manufacturing plant.

MANAGING PROGRESS

This section starts from the premise that an effective schedule has been produced, and that all key project participants know, and have willingly agreed to, what is expected of them.

Project Progressing as a Closed Loop Control System

Project progressing can be regarded as a closed loop control system (which electronic engineers will recognize as a cybernetic feedback control loop). For every instruction issued, the system response has to be monitored and a resulting feedback signal must be generated. Otherwise there will be no way of knowing when corrective actions are needed. The project manager will ensure that these corrective actions take place, so that the control loop is effectively closed. Figure 9.4 illustrates this concept.

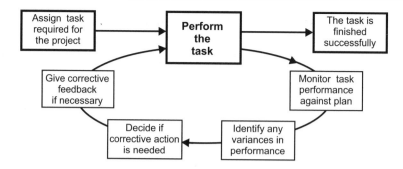

9.4 A cybernetic control loop, an example of management by exception

With any system of control feedback, it is the errors that are significant. In the management context these errors are called 'exceptions' or 'variances'. The sensible approach of concentrating reports and management attention on exceptions is known as 'management by exception'.

There is an alternative management approach for the incompetent or lazy manager. This relies only on outgoing instructions, with no feedback or error signals. This is called 'management by surprise', because the manager feeds in work at one end of the system and is surprised when it doesn't come out at the other!

PROGRESS MONITORING AND SCHEDULE UPDATING

It is the project manager's responsibility to ensure that all other managers in the organization are made aware of project requirements. When any project is in progress it is necessary to have two-way communication between the project manager and every departmental manager. For every work instruction issued, information must be fed back regularly on the resulting progress.

In other words, there must be effective communications.

Case Example of a Communication Failure

There was one occasion when I failed to give essential project schedule information to another manager (H), whose department thus did not carry out their project tasks on time. We were both hauled before our divisional director and H was asked why he had failed. His very reasonable excuse was 'Dennis did not pass the information to me'. I could see the end of my career in sight but was astonished and relieved to hear the director tell H 'It was your job to find out'. H was fired soon after and I never made that mistake again. We learn by our mistakes and I learned then and have since never forgotten the importance of good communications in all projects.

Use of Work-to Lists as Progress Returns

If work instructions are to be conveyed from the project manager to participants by way of work-to lists, there is no reason why the same procedure should not be used in reverse to feed back progress information. The only missing item is a document complementary to the work-to list. This gap can be filled by one of the following:

1. the use of specially designed progress return forms
2. line managers annotating and returning copies of their work-to lists
3. direct input to the project computer or server by managers and supervisors.

Option 1 introduces more forms and clerical work, which should be avoided if possible. For Option 2, Open Plan is an example of a software package that can print a combined work-to list and questionnaire progress return in its standard range of reports. Other packages also allow space for comments on their work-to lists or task lists.

For option 3, it is often practicable for departmental managers (and other trusted people) to access the project computer from their own desks. The project manager will want to be assured that progress information fed directly to the computer in this way emanates from truthful and reasonably senior staff. False input statements could lead to subsequent errors in network analysis, resource scheduling and future work-to lists. If the computer is holding a large, complex multi-project model, the group or person responsible for scheduling will always be wary of any input that could corrupt the model and cause many hours of restoration work.

Although project progress information can be updated continuously, work-to lists and other schedules will often need to be revised and reissued only when the planner decides that this is necessary to keep issued instructions up to date.

Quality and Reliability of Progress Information

Whatever the method used for progress feedback, care must be taken to avoid either ambiguity or undue complication. The simpler the method, the more likely will be the chances of persuading all those responsible to return data regularly on time. Persuading key participants to report progress accurately and on time is not always easy, but project control will break down if this cannot be done.

Nature of Progress Information Required to Update Schedules

Whether the system's progress reporting relies on questionnaires or data input from line managers, the following facts or estimates are usually required for each activity that has been started, finished or worked on since the previous report or keyboard visit:

- If started since the previous report, what was the actual starting date?
- If started but not finished, either:
  - the estimated percentage completion at time-now or;
  - the estimated remaining duration after time-now.
- Is the activity finished?
- If finished, what was the actual finish date?

Time-now means the date entered into the computer from which the next schedule update will be calculated. No tasks or portions of them will be scheduled to take place before this time-now.

Questions of Logic

There is another question that the perceptive project manager needs to know for each task that has been reported as complete. This vital question is: *Can this activity's immediate successor(s) be started?* This is the acid test of whether or not an activity has truly been completed. If the network logic is correct, then an activity cannot strictly be reported as complete if its immediately following tasks cannot be started.

An alert project manager will recognize the danger behind a progress return which says that the percentage progress achieved is 99 or 100 per cent, but that the next activity cannot start. This could mean that the progress claimed has not been made. This anomaly also occurs when a design engineer has completed a batch of drawings, but refuses to release them for issue through lack of confidence in the design, or because he or she feel that (given more time) the drawings could be improved.

Sometimes an activity can be started even though one or more of its predecessors is still in progress. For example, an activity, although not complete, could be sufficiently advanced to allow the release of procurement lists for long-lead items. A network diagram may not always indicate such possibilities, and very often these opportunities for expediting progress would be missed by individuals who had not regularly asked the right questions.

Activities are quite often reported as started before one or more predecessors have been reported as finished. This is in contradiction to the logic enshrined in the network so that, when it happens, it indicates that the network constraints were not absolute. None the less, if that is the situation, then it has to be accepted and reported to the computer accordingly: most software should be capable of accepting 'out of sequence' progress data.

Management by Walking About

The methods described so far for collecting progress information can work properly only in an ideal world. They paint a picture of the project manager sitting behind a desk, issuing instructions and receiving reports while the project proceeds smoothly to its successful finish. While efficient routine systems are commendable and necessary, more is needed. The project manager must be prepared to depart from the routine and their desk from time to time, making visits and spot checks, giving praise or encouragement where due, and viewing physical progress at first hand. This process is sometimes called 'management by walking about'.

Visits to sites or production areas are particularly useful when two or more visits are made some little time apart, so that progress (or lack of it) can be noted. Photographs (particularly at construction sites) can be taken on such visits, both for checking progress and as a permanent record of the project as it develops.

Global Checks

One useful occasional check is to ask how many people in a department (or of a particular staff grade) are currently working on the project. The answer can then be compared with the manpower usage planned for that date.

Comparison of scheduled and actual cost curves can also be made, but the head count is quicker, more positive, and likely to produce the earlier warning. Suppose that 35 design engineers are scheduled to be working on a project on the check date. If only 18 people can be counted, something is obviously very wrong somewhere. Although routine progress returns might indicate that everything is on schedule, the 'head count' shows that work on the project in the design department is not taking place at the required rate.

When action is taken, it may be found that project design is held up for lack of information, that other work has been given priority, or that the department is seriously under-staffed. The project manager must investigate the reason and take steps to set the scheduled number of people to work.

WHEN THE NEWS IS BAD

How Bad?

When jobs start to run late, the first thing that the project manager must do is to consider the effect that this is likely to have on the following:

1. The current project
2. Projects or other work queuing in the organization's pipeline
3. The customer.

On rare occasions, late running might be acceptable and require no action. Usually, however, corrective action is needed. The project manager must then assess the situation, decide the appropriate action and implement it.

Jobs with free float

If a late-running task has enough free float to absorb the delay, all that needs to be done is to ensure that the work is expedited and finished without further interruption, within the available free float.

Jobs with some total float

Total float has to be treated with more circumspection than free float, because total float used up by late working will rob later tasks of their float. So, even jobs that possess total float should be expedited to bring them back on schedule if possible.

Purchasing and other departments have always suffered at the hands of project managers by being expected unfairly to perform miracles when all the total float has been used up long before work enters the purchasing and later phases.

Jobs with zero or negative float

If critical tasks (tasks with zero or negative float) are late, then special measures must be taken. It might be necessary to accept more expensive working methods to expedite these late jobs and bring them back on schedule. If a task expected to cost £1000 is in danger of running several weeks late and jeopardizing the handover date of a project worth £1m, then it might be worth spending £10 000 or even more on the problem task if that could rescue the overall programme. The project manager must always view the costs of expediting individual activities against the benefits gained for the whole project.

Corrective Measures

Corrective measures will only be effective when they are taken in time, which means that adequate warning of problems must be given. This will depend on having a well-prepared schedule, keeping it up to date, and monitoring progress regularly.

Working overtime, perhaps over one or two weekends, can sometimes recover time. The project manager will be relieved, on such occasions, that overtime working was not built into the normal schedules. Used occasionally, overtime can be an effective help in overcoming delays. Used regularly or too often however, the law of diminishing returns will apply, with staff permanently tired and working under fatigue, with no adequate reserves.

If problems are caused by shortage of resources, perhaps these could be made available from external sources by subcontracting. Or, there might be additional capacity somewhere else in the contractor's own organization that could be mobilized.

The network logic should always be re-examined critically. Can some tasks can be overlapped, bypassed or even eliminated?

Special motivational measures, incentives, or even unorthodox actions can sometimes give progress a much needed boost, provided that these measures are not repeated too often and are used sensibly.

In dire circumstances, when many tasks are running late, setting up a task force to drive the remaining work can be an effective solution.

PROGRESS MEETINGS

Any project manager worthy of the title will want to make certain that whenever possible their tactics are preventative rather than curative. If a special meeting can be successful in resolving problems, why not pre-empt trouble by having regular progress meetings, with senior representatives of all departments present?

Regular progress meetings provide a forum where essential dialogue can take place between the project manager, planners and the project participants. The main purpose of progress meetings is to review project progress and find ways of implementing corrective action if programme slippages occur or appear likely.

Frequency of Progress Meetings

The frequency with which meetings are held depends to a large extent on the nature of the project, the size and geographical spread of its organization, and its overall timescale.

On projects of short duration, and with much detail to be considered, there may be a good case for holding progress meetings frequently, say once a week, on an informal basis at supervisor level. For other projects monthly meetings may be adequate. Meetings at relatively junior level can be backed up by less frequent meetings held at more senior level.

Project review meetings, which can cover the financial prospects as well as simple progress, can also be arranged. Senior managers may wish to attend such meetings and for some capital projects the customer might also want to be represented.

Meetings held too frequently create apathy or anger. Departmental supervisors and managers are usually busy people whose time should not be wasted.

Keeping to the Subject

There are dangers associated with the mismanagement of progress meetings. For instance, it often happens that lengthy discussions between specialists concern technical issues that should be resolved outside the meeting. Such discussions can bore the other members of the meeting, waste their scarce and expensive time, and cause rapid loss of interest in the proceedings. It is never possible to divorce technical considerations from progress topics, but design meetings and progress meetings are basically different functions and should be kept apart. Discussions should be kept to progress topics, with irrelevancies swept aside.

Was the Meeting Successful?

When a meeting breaks up, it will have been successful only if all the members feel that they have achieved some real purpose and that actions have been agreed which will benefit the project. Demands made of members during the meeting must be achievable, so that promises extracted can be honoured.

Issuing the Minutes

Minutes must be published without delay, so that they do not become outdated by further events before distribution. Minutes should be clearly and concisely written, combining brevity with clarity, accuracy and careful layout, allowing each action demanded to stand out from the page. If the document is too bulky it may not even be read. Short, pointed statements of fact are all that is required.

No ambiguity must be allowed as to who is directly responsible for taking each agreed action. Every person listed for taking action must receive a copy of the minutes (although this seems obvious, the point is sometimes overlooked). Times must be stated definitively. Expressions such as 'at the end of next week' or 'towards the end of the month' should be discarded in favour of actual dates.

Progress Meetings Abandoned

The above account of progress meetings adheres to the conventional view that progress meetings are an accepted way of project life. Here is some food for less conventional thought.

A heavy engineering company held progress meetings at regular intervals or whenever things looked like going badly wrong. Several projects were in progress at any time, and the permanent engineering department of about 60 people was often augmented by as many as 80 subcontracted staff working either in-house or in external offices.

Meetings typically resulted in excuses from participants as to why actions requested of them at previous meetings had been carried out late or not at all. Each meeting would end with a new set of promises, ready to fuel a fresh collection of excuses at the next meeting. The company's overall record was not particularly bad, but there was room for improvement and time was being wasted through too many meetings.

Senior company management supported a study which led to the introduction of critical path network planning for all projects, using a computer to schedule resources and issue detailed work-to lists. Two progress engineers were engaged, one to follow up in-house work and the other to visit subcontractors. Both these progress engineers had the benefit of work-to lists, which told them exactly which jobs should be in progress at any time, the scheduled start and finish dates for those jobs, how many people should be working on each of them, how many people should be working in total on each project at any time and the amount of float left for every activity.

By following up activities on a day-by-day basis from the work-to lists, these two progress engineers succeeded in achieving a considerable improvement in progress and the smooth flow of work. If a critical or near-critical activity looked like running late, stops were pulled out to bring it back into line (occasionally by working overtime during evenings and weekends if necessary). Fortunately, all the staff were cooperative, grateful (in fact) for the new sense of order created in their working lives.

After a few months under this new system it dawned on managers that they were no longer being asked to attend progress meetings. Except for kick-off meetings at the introduction of new projects, progress meetings had become unnecessary.

PROJECT PROGRESS REPORTS

Internal Reports to Company Management

Progress reports to company management must give the technical, fulfilment and financial status of the project and compare performance in each of these respects with the scheduled requirements. For projects lasting more than a few months, such reports are usually issued at regular intervals. For many reasons it is important that data on the condition and management of the project are presented factually, supported where necessary by carefully reasoned predictions or explanations.

Information in these internal reports may contain detailed information of a proprietary nature. They might, therefore, have to be treated as confidential, with their distribution restricted to a limited number of people, all within the company.

Exception Reports

There is another type of internal management report in addition to the detailed management reports just described. These are the reports of exceptions, and are confined to those project factors which give rise to acute concern, and which demand immediate attention.

If the report is to do with costs, the exceptions will probably be called 'variances', which is the term used by accountants.

Exception reports can be contained in documents such as cost reports, materials shortage lists or computer printouts of jobs running late. At the other extreme, an exception report might be the frenzied beating on a senior manager's door by a distraught project manager who feels that their project and world have fallen apart.

Before allowing any exception report to be passed to more senior management, the project manager must be certain that some remedy within their own control cannot be found. However, once it has been established that events are moving out of control, the project manager must tell senior management without delay.

All of this is, of course, following the sensible practice of management by exception. This seeks to prevent senior managers from being bombarded with large volumes of routine information that should be of concern only to supervisors and junior managers. The intention is to leave executives free to concentrate their efforts on strategic issues, not on day-to-day issues.

Reports to the Client or Customer

Sending formal progress reports to the client or customer is often a condition of contract. If the customer expects regular reports then, clearly, these can be derived from the same source which compiled the internal management reports. Some of the more detailed technical information in the internal reports may not be of interest to the customer or relevant to its needs. Customer progress reports, therefore, are usually based on internal management reports, with suitable editing.

Whether or not project financial reports are to be attached to customers' progress reports will depend on the contractor's role in each case. Under some circumstances cost and profitability predictions must be regarded as proprietary information, not to be disclosed outside the company. In other cases, the project manager may have to submit cost summaries or more detailed breakdowns and forecasts.

Although customer reports may be edited to improve clarity and remove proprietary information, they must never be allowed intentionally to mislead. It is always important to keep the customer informed of the true progress position, especially when slippages have occurred which cannot be contained within the available float. Any attempt to put off the evil day by placating a customer with optimistic forecasts or unfounded promises must lead to unwelcome repercussions eventually. Nobody likes to discover that they have been taken for a ride, and customers are no exception to this rule.

10 *Managing Purchasing*

The total cost of purchased goods and services exceeds half the total costs of most projects and can even be as high as 80 per cent. Thus efficient purchasing is essential for the success of any project. Delays caused by materials shortages or purchasing errors can damage a project, causing work interruption, delays and expensive idle time.

OUTLINE OF THE PURCHASING FUNCTION

Purchasing is part of a wider materials management function that can include vendor appraisal, contract negotiation, freight, goods inwards inspection and the safe handling and storage of goods received. It extends beyond the boundaries of the purchaser's premises to include supervisory expediting and inspection visits to suppliers, packing and transport arrangements, port and customers clearance for international movements, and involvement whenever special provisions have to be made for insurance, credit guarantees and other commercial arrangements.

The purchase of a high-cost item can often be regarded as a mini-project in itself. The process is usually cyclical, because it begins and ends with the buyer. Just as a project has a life cycle, so does the purchase of a significant item for a project. Compare the purchasing cycle in Figure 10.1 with the project cycle shown earlier in Figure 1.1.

In this chapter the word 'buyer' is used to describe the person or group responsible directly for the purchasing function. This might be a purchasing agent, purchasing manager or a suitably experienced buying clerk in a purchasing department. The organization that supplies the goods might be known as the supplier or the vendor, and might be the manufacturer of the goods or a stockist or agent.

Methods will depend to a large extent on the type of industry and the nature of the goods being purchased. At one end of the scale is the urgent item obtained by sending someone to the nearest hardware store with some petty cash. At the other extreme is the purchase of a complex piece of capital plant or an enormous bulk purchase of materials. Figure 10.2 lists purchasing procedures applicable to many projects. In this figure, items ranged to the left would apply to low-cost purchases, while those to the right of the illustration would be needed only for buying high-

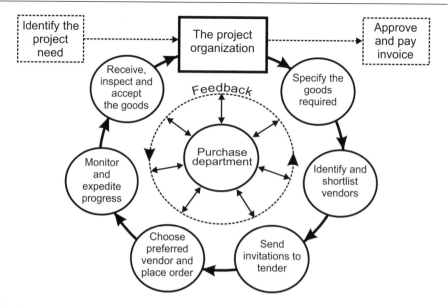

10.1 Purchasing cycle for a high-value project item

cost items, including those needing special import-export documentation and international freight procedures.

SPECIFYING THE GOODS TO BE PURCHASED

The first step in purchasing is to specify the requirements. In many projects, this function is often the responsibility of a project engineer or designer.

Parts lists or purchase control schedules are often used to list all the requirements. Both methods are similar and require the engineer to list each item, give the quantity required, and add a description and a specification or catalogue number. The correct revision status of all specifications must be given.

In construction and civil engineering projects the quantities of bulk construction materials required are listed on take-off lists.

Sometimes a relevant standards specification will exist that can be quoted to specify the requirements of a purchase. There are some specifications provided by official bodies, including the armed services.

Bought-out parts, equipment and materials can often be specified by reference to a manufacturer's catalogue or part number. This might seem to be a sufficiently rigid description of the goods. However, most manufacturers reserve the right to modify their designs. If goods are supplied by a stockist, that stockist might decide to restock from more than one manufacturer, and there might be significant differences in the materials quality or design.

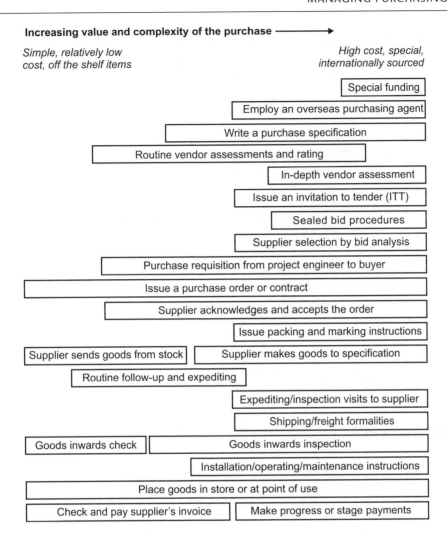

Increasing value and complexity of the purchase ⟶

Simple, relatively low cost, off the shelf items

High cost, special, internationally sourced

Special funding

Employ an overseas purchasing agent

Write a purchase specification

Routine vendor assessments and rating

In-depth vendor assessment

Issue an invitation to tender (ITT)

Sealed bid procedures

Supplier selection by bid analysis

Purchase requisition from project engineer to buyer

Issue a purchase order or contract

Supplier acknowledges and accepts the order

Issue packing and marking instructions

Supplier sends goods from stock | Supplier makes goods to specification

Routine follow-up and expediting

Expediting/inspection visits to supplier

Shipping/freight formalities

Goods inwards check | Goods inwards inspection

Installation/operating/maintenance instructions

Place goods in store or at point of use

Check and pay supplier's invoice | Make progress or stage payments

10.2 Some purchasing procedures applicable to projects

Some companies take no chances and produce their own drawings and specifications and allocate part numbers themselves. This practice costs engineering time, but has much to commend it. Apart from removing any ambiguity about what is being ordered, provision is thus made for a common part-numbering system. That simplifies purchasing procedures, stock handling, stores procedures and cost accounting.

The project engineers must always write a detailed purchase specification for complex or specially manufactured goods or for any item that could give rise to safety and reliability difficulties if it were to be incorrectly supplied. Companies with good project experience will keep outline specifications in their digital files, greatly reducing the design or engineering time and effort to write a particular purchase specification.

EARLY ORDERING OF LONG-LEAD ITEMS

Engineers and others responsible for initiating project purchases have a duty to inform the purchasing department of goods that are likely to have long lead times. They must ensure that ordering instructions are passed to the purchasing department as soon as possible. This often means issuing advance information on such things as special bearings, castings, motors and other bought-out components, although the relevant assembly drawings and final bills of material or purchase schedules remain unfinished or even unstarted.

It is sometimes desirable to issue advance information, even when the goods cannot be specified in exact detail, to allow the purchasing department to get provisional quotations from suppliers. In a really urgent case the buyer can reserve capacity in a manufacturer's works by issuing a letter of intent.

Some engineers have a dangerous tendency to contact potential suppliers directly on matters that could lead to verbal contracts being made. Of course there will be many times when designers and engineers need to speak to suppliers on technical issues but care must always be taken to leave discussions on contractual matters to the purchasing department.

CHOOSING THE BEST SUPPLIER

The buyer's first responsibility is to select a suitable supplier. Occasionally only one supplier can be found, or one may be specified as the preferred supplier on the project engineer's requisition.

There are, of course, occasions when urgency is the most important factor, when there is simply no time in which to conduct a thorough supplier selection procedure. In all other cases, the supplier should be chosen after the collection and perusal of several competitive quotations.

Purchase Enquiries and Invitations to Tender

Whenever competitive quotations are required, the engineers must help the buyer to compile a bid package. This package will include the technical specification and commercial needs of the project. The engineers might have a preferred supplier, or a shortlist of possible suppliers. Buyers in the purchasing department will usually have their own knowledge of the market and might know of others who should be approached.

Obtaining bids

For high-cost purchases items the procedures are often very rigid, with strict procedures for issuing invitations to tender (ITT) and methods for receiving and assessing the resulting bids.

Purchases and contracts for projects in the public sector above specified threshold values are subject to special directives within the EU, which can add months to the purchasing process. The intention of these directives is to achieve fair competition and work opportunities throughout the EU. Opportunities for new contracts may not be advertised in the UK before a contract notice has been published in the *Official Journal of the EU*. There are exceptions for contracts for secret work.

Sealed bids

The buyer might wish to obtain bids according to a sealed bids procedure. The process is outlined in the sequence shown in Figure 10.3.

Potential suppliers might be asked to present their sealed bids in two separate packages, one technical and the other commercial. The buyer (in collaboration with the relevant project engineer) will open all the technical bids first and the project engineer will reject those that fail to meet the specification. Then the surviving commercial bids are opened and compared.

In many cases there will be dialogue or negotiation between bidders and the buyer during the bidding period. These discussions can obviously influence the final prices and deliveries quoted. It is important not to give any supplier an unfair advantage during such discussions by revealing information not available to the other competitors. The ITT procedure will usually ensure that when a bidder asks a question or seeks clarification, both the bidder's question and the buyer's answer will be made known to all the other bidders.

Bid summary and evaluation

Potential suppliers might be in different countries, using their own national currencies, with very different journeys and transport methods needed to get the goods to the project site. The buyer will need to deal with all these variables so that the bids can be compared on a similar basis. A bid summary form can be used for that purpose.

A bid summary example is shown in Figure 10.4. This is intended to convert all bids into one common currency, and to include all required items that some bidders might quote as optional extras. Estimated packing, carriage, insurance, port and customs costs arising from foreign bidders have to be included. This procedure helps to ensure that the total delivered costs at the project point of use are compared for all potential suppliers on a like-for-like basis.

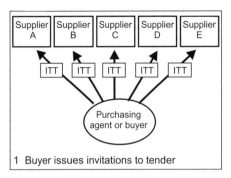

1 Buyer issues invitations to tender

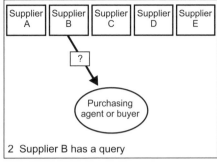

2 Supplier B has a query

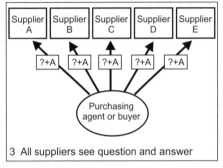

3 All suppliers see question and answer

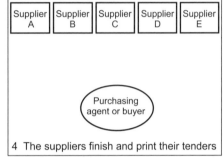

4 The suppliers finish and print their tenders

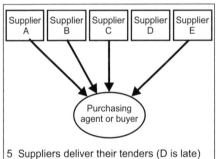

5 Suppliers deliver their tenders (D is late)

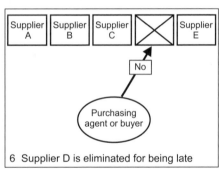

6 Supplier D is eliminated for being late

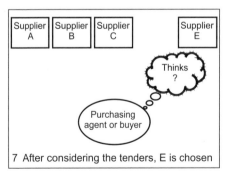

7 After considering the tenders, E is chosen

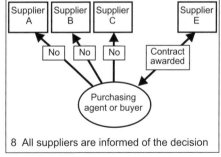

8 All suppliers are informed of the decision

10.3 A typical sealed bids process

BID SUMMARY

SELLERS ⟶			A	B	C	D	E	F
Country of origin								
Bid reference								
Bid date								
Period of validity								
Bid currency								
Project exchange rate								
Item	Qty	Description	Price	Price	Price	Price	Price	Price
Total quoted ex-works								
Discounts (if any)								
Packing and export prep cost								
Shipping cost								
Customs duty and tax								
Local transport cost								
Estimated total cost on site								
Delivery time ex-works								
Estimated total transport time								
Total delivery time to sit								

RECOMMENDED BY THE PURCHASING AGENT:

....

For purchasing agent

RECOMMENDED BY THE ENGINEER:

....

Project/ senior engineer

RECOMMENDATION TO THE CLIENT:

....

Project manager

Specification title:	Specification number:

10.4   A bid summary example

The buyer would usually be expected to favour the lowest bidder, but this choice must be tempered by the bidder's reputation for quality, delivery performance and commercial standing.

It is usually undesirable to allow the buyer to choose a supplier without technical evaluation and agreement from the relevant project engineer. The bid summary form illustrated in Figure 10.4 is not intended to record all the details of such technical deliberations.

Responsibility for shipping goods

It is important that the boundaries of responsibility for transportation are clearly defined in bids and on purchase orders. Incoterms, defined and published in many languages by the International Chamber of Commerce, are accepted worldwide as the succinct and definitive method for setting out these boundaries.

International freight movements for projects can involve complex procedures. Unless the purchasing department is thoroughly familiar with these, a freight forwarding agent should be used.

PURCHASE ORDER

Authority for the buyer to make a purchase is often initiated by the issue of a purchase requisition to the buyer by the project engineer (or other nominated person from the project team). For purchases of significant size or complexity, the requisition can comprise two parts:

1. The technical specification, which the buyer will subsequently forward to the chosen supplier as an attachment to a purchase order.
2. The commercial specification. This might be an informal note provided by the engineer advising the purchasing department of things such as the project budget and delivery requirements. Thus this could include confidential comments or instructions from the engineer to the buyer that are not intended for passing on to the chosen supplier. However, the buyer will take this commercial specification into account when preparing the purchase order and its conditions of contract.

Issuing the purchase order is perceived as the most routine and obvious part of the purchasing function. Typically, it involves completing a purchase order form, adding an authorizing signature, and sending it to the supplier, together with any supporting drawings and the technical specification. A standard purchase order form should normally be used, although that may not be possible when ordering online. The information on a purchase order usually comprises:

- A purchase order serial number (for identification and subsequent information retrieval).
- The description and name of the goods to be supplied.
- The quantity required.
- The agreed purchase price, as quoted by the supplier and accepted by the purchaser.
- The delivery date required.
- The reference number and date of the supplier's quotation (or catalogue number of the goods).
- The address to which the goods are to be delivered.
- The terms (Incoterms) on which delivery is to be made. This will show liability for transport, packing, insurance costs, and so on.
- Invoicing instructions.
- An authorizing signature.

The project time schedule must always allow time for the preparation and issue of purchase orders. Unless emergency measures are contemplated, two weeks should often be regarded as a minimum estimate for purchase lead time, even for items that can be supplied from a supplier's stock. Purchase lead times should be shown as tasks on network diagrams.

Contractual Conditions

One aspect that should concern the project manager is that each purchase order sets out commercial conditions which, once accepted by the supplier as a contract, commit the buyer (and therefore the project) to all implied cost and legal implications. It is customary for companies to standardize their usual commercial conditions of purchase and print them on the reverse of their purchase order forms.

After receiving the purchase order, the chosen supplier will be expected to return an acknowledgement accepting the terms, or at least confirming details of quantity, description, price and delivery. Naturally these details must be compared with the supplier's original quotation, and the buyer will question any discrepancy. When the order has been accepted by the supplier, a binding legal contract exists.

Purchase Order Amendments

Should it become necessary to change any aspect of a purchase order after issue, the supplier's agreement should be sought to determine the effect on price and delivery, and to ensure that the proposed change is within the supplier's capability. Once these facts have been successfully established, an amendment to the original purchase order must be issued.

Each purchase order amendment should bear the same serial number as the original purchase order, suffixed by an identifying amendment number (amendment

1, 2, 3 etc.). Purchase order amendments should be given the same distribution as the original purchase orders.

EXPEDITING

For purchases where the delivery waiting time is more than a few weeks the buyer will usually make routine checks with the supplier to ensure that no delivery delay will occur.

For some complex or high-value equipment, especially where this is manufactured specially to order, the purchaser might wish to send an inspector or expediter to the supplier's premises to witness progress at first hand.

Inspection and Expediting Visits

The buyer might wish to arrange visits to a supplier's premises to check on progress, inspect workmanship or witness tests. Such visits could be linked to the certification of stage payments. This is a function where overseas purchasing agents can be most useful when dealing with offshore suppliers.

There are several ways in which responsibility for carrying out inspection and expediting visits can be allocated or delegated. Where suitable engineers are available to the purchase agent concerned, it is often convenient to arrange visits which combine the inspection and estimating functions.

For purchases from overseas suppliers the project purchaser might employ an overseas purchasing agent who is based within practicable reach of the supplier. That agent can then represent the project contractor by carrying out local inspection and expediting visits.

The project manager (and possibly the client) will expect to see a quality and progress report from the relevant purchasing agent following each visit to a supplier. The inspecting engineer or expediter will probably be asked to use a convenient standard summary form for this purpose, an example of which is given in Figure 10.5.

Alternative Sourcing

If expediting appears to be failing, the design engineers might be able to suggest an alternative item that can be obtained more quickly. The solution might mean finding another source of supply. If the original order does have to be cancelled because the supplier has failed to make the agreed delivery, there should be no kickback, because the supplier has broken the contract by failing to perform.

INSPECTION/EXPEDITING REPORT

Report number	Sheet 1 of	Date this visit	Date of last visit	Inspector/expediter

MAIN SUPPLIER DETAILS

Name _____

Address _____

_____

Supplier's reference _____

Persons contacted _____

_____

Equipment _____

_____

_____

_____

Contract delivery date

Current delivery estimate

Plans for next visit

Date _____

To expedite ☐

To continue inspection ☐

Final inspection ☐

To inspect packing ☐

SUB-SUPPLIER DETAILS

Main supplier's order number _____

Name _____

Address _____

_____

Sub-supplier's reference _____

Persons contacted _____

_____

Equipment _____

_____

Agreed delivery to supplier

Current delivery estimate

Plans for next visit

Date _____

To expedite ☐

To continue inspection ☐

Final inspection ☐

To inspect packing ☐

ORDER STATUS SUMMARY (see attached sheets for details)

Assessed progress by (weeks)	Tests witnessed?	Complies with specification?	Released for packing?	Released for shipping?
Early ☐	Yes ☐	Yes ☐	Yes ☐	Yes ☐
Late ☐	No ☐	No ☐	No ☐	No ☐

ACTION REQUIRED	ACTION BY
	Specification No / Revision
Title	Purchase order No / Amendment

10.5 An inspection and expediting report example

SHIPPING, PORT AND CUSTOMS FORMALITIES

Marking and Labelling

The purchasing agent must ensure that every consignment is properly marked before it leaves the supplier's premises. The marking method required should be stated on the purchase specification, and will usually involve suppliers stencilling easily recognizable markings on packing crates so that each item can be clearly identified through all stages of its journey and, not least, by the site personnel when it finally arrives. The purchase order number usually has to be included in all markings.

Freight Forwarding Agents

It is best to entrust arrangements for long-distance transport, shipping, airfreight, seaport and airport and international frontier formalities to a specialist organization. The purchasing agent will undoubtedly have considerable experience and expertise, but the employment of a reputable freight forwarding agent will be invaluable.

Freight forwarding agents operate through worldwide organizations. They have their staff or representatives stationed at or near many of the world's ports and airports. They are able to monitor the progress of every consignment through all stages from initial loading to final delivery.

Collaboration between the purchasing agent and a freight forwarding agent can achieve benefits from the economy of scale obtained when different consignments are consolidated to make up complete container loads.

The combined expertise of the purchasing and freight forward agent can be a great comfort to project staff confronted for the first time with the need to deal with the formidable array of documents associated with the international movement of goods. Failure to get the documentation right first time can lead to delays, the impounding of goods, and to legally imposed penalties.

Local knowledge provided by the forwarding agent's contacts in the countries along the delivery route can yield important information about the type and capacity of port handling facilities, warning of any unusual congestion or industrial disputes (with suggestions for alternative routes), and details of inland road and rail systems (including size and weight restrictions). For example, the agent in one case was able to prevent an expensive mistake by pointing out that a local railway company operated an unusually short restriction on the maximum length of loads, because the route included tunnels with unusually sharp curves. At another port, the local agents were able to warn about a peculiar security problem, where the local shanty-town inhabitants were always on the lookout for fresh supplies of building timber. If such timber happened to exist in the shape of well-constructed packing crates protecting expensive project equipment standing on the dockside – well, who could blame them?

GOODS RECEIPT

Receipt of the goods is not the end of the story. Each consignment must be examined on receipt to check for possible loss or damage in transit. There might also have been some mistake, either in the quantity supplied or in the nature of the goods. This applies where the goods are to be delivered to the contractor's premises or to a construction site managed by the contractor.

Goods inwards inspectors may wish to examine the goods more thoroughly to ensure that they comply with requirements although, in recent years, the tendency has been to place more reliance on the suppliers' own quality procedures.

If the goods are accepted, the goods inwards personnel will usually issue a goods inwards certificate. The issue of a goods inwards certificate has several purposes. It is often the signal to the accounts department that they can release payment of the supplier's invoice, although a counter signature from the project manager might also be needed.

If a consignment is not received in satisfactory condition it will be sent smartly back whence it came accompanied by an explanatory rejection note. Rejection notes produce opposite reactions to those caused by goods inwards certificates. For example, the accounts department will not pay the supplier's invoice, and the purchasing department will redouble its expediting efforts.

SHORTAGES

Project tasks are sometimes delayed because of materials shortages or have to be started before all the necessary materials have been received. Shortages arise through breakages, theft, inadequate general stock levels, purchasing mistakes, late delivery from suppliers and a variety of other reasons.

Shortage Lists

No project manager likes to see any job delayed because of shortages. A method often used to deal with shortages depends on the issue of shortage lists. These documents can be used for all kinds of projects – for factory materials or for shortages on a construction site for example. A shortage list is the personification of management by exception. It should:

- be quick and simple for the manager or supervisor of the job affected to use;
- describe the missing materials by type and quantity;
- provide precise, unambiguous information to the person responsible for purchasing so that the purchase order can be identified, allowing the supplier to be contacted and chased.

In addition, a shortage list system should:

- indicate the degree of urgency;
- allow information feedback, so that the manager or supervisor involved can be told when to expect delivery.

The essential elements of a shortage list are illustrated in Figure 10.6.

Materials shortage report			
Project:		Date:	
Department:		Issued by:	
To the purchasing manager. The following items have not been received. Please expedite and report back.		Is work held up? Yes or no ⟶	
Order number (if known)	Description	Quantity needed	Reply from purchasing manager

10.6   Example of a materials shortage list

VENDORS' DOCUMENTS

Provision must usually be made for the project engineers to receive and approve documents from the suppliers of machinery or equipment which is manufactured specially for the project. The term 'vendors' documents' is usually applied, although the providers of the goods might also be referred to as manufacturers, sellers, suppliers or subcontractors.

The first step in ensuring the timely receipt of vendors' documents is to make certain that the obligations for providing them are spelled out clearly on the purchase orders or purchase specifications.

When the equipment is delivered, a final set of drawings, certified test results, operating and maintenance manuals and a recommended spares holding list will be needed for some machinery or other manufactured equipment. In some cases, suppliers might be required to supply all these documents translated into a foreign language, according to the nationality of the project end user.

Foundation, Capacity and Installation Drawings

In addition to general layout or assembly drawings, there is usually a requirement for the early receipt of installation instructions. For example, heavy plant and machinery might require foundation drawings, power supply requirements and overall weights and dimensions, the lack of which could hold up work on the project. Obtaining such information, and progressing any necessary approvals, is all part of the essential expediting process.

Retention of Vendors' Documents

The project engineering company will have obligations in providing a back-up service to the client after project handover. These obligations usually extend beyond the initial guarantee period, and can involve the provision of advice or services in maintaining, repairing, replacing, operating, modifying or extending plant or buildings provided for the original project.

Since much of the plant in an industrial project will incorporate equipment purchased from third-party suppliers, the contractor must be able to find and consult any relevant vendor document for many years after project completion if good post-project service is to be given. The contractor will therefore need to keep a complete project set of vendors' documentation safely in its own files or archives (either in their original paper state, or on some other medium of suitable quality and durability).

It is not sufficient to rely on being able to obtain additional or replacement copies from all the various suppliers in the future. The commercial world is a volatile place. Some original suppliers might lose or destroy their records, be swallowed up in mergers or takeovers, or simply cease trading.

11 *Managing Changes*

Projects seldom run from start to finish without at least one change. Changes can arise from a customer's request, a self-inflicted design modification, or through the project having to depart in some respect from the officially issued drawings, specifications or other issued instructions.

THE IMPACT OF CHANGES IN RELATION TO THE PROJECT LIFE CYCLE

Changes generally disrupt a project more and cost more to implement when they are made later in the project life cycle. This is illustrated in Figure 11.1.

Suppose a change is made when the project is in its early planning or business case stage. No actual work on the project has been done. The change might cause delay but the only material things that need changing are the documents which set out the business case or the project specification. Of course time spent in meetings and discussions costs money, and thus the change would increase early management costs, but those costs are likely to be insignificant compared with the costs of the actual project.

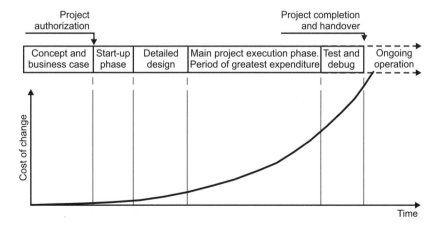

11.1   The cost of a change in relation to the project life cycle

Now suppose that a change has to be made after work on a project has begun. That could cause work done earlier to be scrapped. Some sunk costs will have to be written off, and project completion could be delayed. A significant change when a project is nearing completion could even be disastrous.

So, although all change proposals always have to be considered seriously, they become far more potentially damaging as the project progresses through its life cycle.

CLASSIFICATION OF CHANGES

Changes can be placed in one of two principal commercial categories, which are *funded* or *unfunded*. The crucial question is: 'Did the customer ask for this change or was it our own fault?' The answer will usually determine whether or not the resulting costs will be paid for by the customer.

External, Customer-requested Changes

Changes requested by the customer should automatically suggest a change to the contract, since the original and specification forms part of the contract documentation. If the change causes an increase in the contractor's costs, a suitable addition to the contract price must be negotiated. The delivery schedule might also be affected and any resulting delays must be assessed, discussed and agreed.

Customer-funded modifications usually possess nuisance value and can disrupt the smooth flow of logically planned work. They do nevertheless offer the prospect of compensation through an increase in price and profit. When a customer asks for a change, the contractor is in a strong price-bargaining position because there is no competitor.

Internal, Unfunded Changes

If a contractor finds it necessary to introduce changes itself, the customer cannot be expected to pay (unless the change can be attributed to a specific contingency for which provision was made in the original project contract). The contractor must be prepared to carry the additional costs, write off any work that has to be scrapped and answer to the customer for any resulting delays. For this reason contractors have to be particularly careful when considering and approving unfunded changes.

CHANGE AUTHORIZATION PROCEDURES

The effects of any change, whether customer-requested or not, may be felt far beyond the confines of the project tasks that are directly affected. This could be true of the technical, timescale or cost aspects. A project has to be regarded as a technical and commercial system, in which a change to one part can react with other parts of the system, bringing about consequences that the change's originator may not have been able to foresee. For these reasons alone it is prudent to ensure that every proposed change is considered by at least one key member from every project department, so that the likely overall effects can be predicted as reliably as possible. Naturally these considerations should take place before any change is authorized and put into practice.

Change Committee

In many project organizations a regular panel of experts is appointed to consider changes and decide how they are to be handled. This is often called a change committee or a change board.

A change committee should include those who are able to assess the safety, reliability, performance, cost and timescale consequences of each proposed change. For any proposed change, the committee will have to consider the effects on work-in-progress, and the feasibility of introducing the change into the project.

In projects involving the nuclear industry, aviation, defence or other cases where reliability, safety or performance assume great significance, two key members of a typical change committee represent:

- the *design authority* (typically a chief engineer or chief designer)
- the *inspecting authority* (a person such as a quality assurance manager) who should be able to make assessments on the basis of quality alone, without any commercial pressure.

On large projects, change committees will probably meet on a regular basis, dealing with change requests in batches. Meetings can sometimes be avoided by distributing requests around the committee members, so that each member considers the effect of the proposed change on their area of responsibility.

Decision Criteria

Points which have to be examined by a change committee include the following:

- Is the change actually possible to make?
- Is it a customer-requested or a self-inflicted change?
- What is the estimated cost of the change?
- Will the customer pay? If so, what should be the price?
- If the change is not customer-requested, is it really necessary? Why?
- What will be the effect on progress?
- How will safety, reliability and performance be affected?
- If several identical sets of equipment are being produced, at what point in the production sequence or batch should the change be introduced?

- Will scrap or redundant materials be created?
- Are any items to be changed retrospectively? Are these:
    - In production or construction?
    - In stock?
    - Already delivered to the customer?
- What drawings, specifications and other documents will have to be modified?

When the committee has considered all these questions, it has the following options:

- authorize the change as requested;
- authorize the change with specified limitations;
- refer the request back to the originator (or elsewhere) asking for clarification, or for an alternative solution;
- reject the change, giving reasons and informing the change originator.

REGISTRATION AND PROGRESSING

In any project organization where changes are expected (which really means all project organizations) it is advisable to nominate a change coordinating clerk. This is not usually a full-time role, and the person chosen will probably carry out other project work. The change coordinating clerk may reside in a contracts office, a project management office (PMO), the design department, or elsewhere. The clerk's duties are likely to include:

- registering each change request and allocating a serial number to it;
- distributing the change request;
- following up to ensure that every request is considered by the change committee without avoidable delay;
- following up to ensure that authorized changes are carried out and that all drawings and specifications affected by the change are updated and reissued:
- keeping change archives.

Change registers should highlight requests that are with the change committee for consideration or which are otherwise still 'active'. The clerk can then monitor all outstanding change requests to prevent delays. A final column on the register will usually show each change to be signed off as either implemented or rejected.

FORMAL PROCEDURES FOR EXTERNAL CHANGE REQUESTS

Changes requested by the customer which affect price, delivery or any other aspect of the original purchase order or contract require formal documentation. This documentation should fulfil the following functions:

- describe the change;
- amend the original purchase order or contract;
- inform the project staff and authorize the change;
- show any price change;
- define or predict any change to the project completion date.

Project variation order		PVO number:
		Project number:
Project title:		Issue date:
Summary of change (use continuation sheets if necessary):		
Originator:	Date:	
Effect on project schedule:		
Effect on costs and price:	Cost estimate ref:	
Customer's authorization details:	Our authorization:	
Distribution:		

11.2   Project variation order

Where the original contract was in the form of a purchase order, the customer will usually request a change by issuing a purchase order amendment. In other cases, especially for projects involving construction, changes are recorded on contract variation orders (sometimes called 'project variations' or 'contract variations'). An example is given in Figure 11.2. Similar changes arranged by a main contractor with site construction subcontractors are often known as site variation orders.

Commercial Administration of Customer Changes

On a large project it is likely that a significant number of formal project variations and informal change requests will be received from the customer or client. Some of these changes might require a great deal of discussion before they can be agreed and implemented.

It is easy to appreciate that complications can develop on a large project spanning a long time. There will be changes already agreed and implemented, others agreed but not yet implemented, some being negotiated and perhaps a few that are giving rise to argument or even dispute.

The way in which any individual case is handled is likely to be the responsibility of the contractor's commercial or contracts department (or the legal department if things start to get out of hand). However, the project manager is responsible for achieving the project objectives and, obviously, has to keep track of what those objectives actually are. This can be difficult when changes are many, complex and at different stages of agreement.

It is important, therefore, to maintain an up-to-date log of all customer changes and to make certain that this log accurately records their combined effect on the project specification, scope, budget, and price. This task is often assigned to one or more people in a PMO. It should be possible to consult the log at any time to identify the following:

- all changes requested by the customer up to the current time;
- the relevant contract variation or purchase order amendment number in every case;
- the status of each change, that is whether it has been:
  - agreed;
  - priced (with details);
  - implemented;
  - invoiced.
- the total current change in project price resulting from changes that have been agreed with the customer.

In very complex cases, a change log can act as the file index for all the supporting records of meetings, correspondence and technical documents.

Very large sums of money, considerable time delays and matters of professional competence or liability can be bound up in all these changes. If a system for logging and progressing changes is not put in place at the start of a project, the situation can easily become very confused and put the contractor at commercial and legal risk.

FORMAL PROCEDURE FOR INTERNAL CHANGE REQUESTS

When a designer, in a fit of rage or despair, tears up a drawing or clears the computer and starts again, there is obviously no need to invoke a formal change engineering procedure. Any new design might have to undergo many changes before it is committed to a fully checked and issued drawing. This is all part of the normal, creative development process. Provided that the design intentions remain within the requirements of the design specification, any internal changes made before drawings are formally issued are not generally considered to be modifications or engineering changes.

Some companies circulate early, pre-issue drawings for discussion, advance information or approval. These issues are often distinguished from the fully released versions by labelling them as revision A, revision B, and so on, changing the revision numbers to the series 0, 1, 2 and so on to denote official releases. A rule might, therefore, be suggested that formal engineering change procedures need only be applied to drawing revisions made after the first issue for manufacturing or construction.

Another reason for invoking formal procedures is found whenever there is an intention to depart from the design specification, especially when the development work is being carried out for an external customer. This, again, is a case for using the formal change procedure before any drawing has been issued for manufacture or construction.

Some rule or criterion is needed to determine at which point in the design process the formal change procedure should be introduced. The question to be asked is 'Will the proposed change affect any instruction, specification, plan or budget that has already been issued and agreed with other departments, the customer, or other external organization?' If the answer to this question is 'Yes', the probability is that formal change committee approval will be needed.

Change Request Forms

Individuals should always be asked to put their change requests in writing to the change committee. A standard form should be used, designed in such a way that the originator is induced to answer in advance all the questions that the change committee will usually want to ask. An example is shown in Figure 11.3. Change requests of this type are used widely in engineering projects, although they may be known by different titles, invariably abbreviated to sets of initials. Here are some examples:

ECR – engineering change request
ECO – engineering change order
MR – modification request

The purpose of an engineering change request is to describe, document and seek formal permission for a permanent design change. The change may be unfunded, or it might be the result of a contract variation order and, therefore, funded by the customer.

Any person should be allowed to originate an engineering change request, because it can have no effect until it has been authorized. The method for completing the form should be self-evident from Figure 11.3.

```
┌─────────────────────────────────────────────────────────────────────┐
│ Engineering change request              ECR number:                   │
│ Project title:                          Project number:               │
├───────────────────────────────────────────────────────────────────────┤
│ Details of change requested (use continuation sheets if necessary):   │
│                                                                         │
│                                                                         │
│                                                                         │
├───────────────────────────────────────────────────────────────────────┤
│ Drawings and other documents affected:                                 │
│                                                                         │
├───────────────────────────────────────────────────────────────────────┤
│ Reason for request:                                                     │
│                                                                         │
│ Originator:                             Date:                           │
├───────────────────────────────────────────────────────────────────────┤
│ Emergency action requested (if any):                                   │
│                                                                         │
├───────────────────────────────────────────────────────────────────────┤
│ Effect on costs:              Cost estimate ref:                        │
│                                                                         │
│ Will customer pay, yes ☐  no ☐    If yes, customer authorization ref:  │
├───────────────────────────────────────────────────────────────────────┤
│ Effect on project schedule?                                             │
│                                                                         │
├───────────────────────────────────────────────────────────────────────┤
│ COMMITTEE INSTRUCTIONS: CHANGE APPROVED ☐    NOT APPROVED ☐            │
│ Point of embodiment, stocks, work in progress, units in service, special restrictions etc: │
│                                                                         │
│ Authorized by:                          Date:                           │
└───────────────────────────────────────────────────────────────────────┘
```

11.3 An engineering change request

DESIGN FREEZE

Sometimes project organizations recognize that there is a point in the design and construction of a project after which any change would be particularly inconvenient or damaging. This leads to the announcement of a 'design freeze', or the declaration of a 'stable design' condition, after which the change committee will refuse to consider any change request unless there are compelling reasons, such as safety or a customer request. Ideally the customer should agree to be bound by the design freeze.

THE INTERCHANGEABILITY RULE

The usual practice when a drawing is changed is to re-issue it with a new revision number. If, however, a change results in a manufactured component or assembly being different from other items with which it was previously interchangeable, it is not sufficient merely to change the drawing revision number. The drawing number itself (and therefore the part number) must also be changed.

This is a golden rule to which no exception should ever be allowed, whether the item is a small component or a big assembly.

Example

Suppose that a project requires the use of 1000 small brass spacers, part number 5678. Then, after 500 had been produced in brass the design was cheapened to use mild steel. These brass and steel spacers are interchangeable, and the part number need not be changed. So the drawing for the steel spacers would still be 5678, but it would have to be given a new revision number.

Now suppose that the design had been changed instead to moulded nylon because on some later manufactured assemblies it became necessary for the spacers to be electrically insulating. Because the metal spacers numbered 5678 can no longer be used on all assemblies, the nylon spacers cannot be called part number 5678. They must be given a new distinguishing drawing and part number.

EMERGENCY MODIFICATIONS

We live in an impatient age, and project time can usually be regarded as a scarce commodity. If the need for an essential modification is discovered during the active production phase of a programme, there may simply be no time available in which to issue suitably changed drawings. There are right and wrong ways of dealing with this situation and the following case is an example of the latter.

Case Example – the Kosy-Kwik Company

The project setting

Kosy-Kwik was a company which specialized in the design, supply and installation of heating and air-conditioning systems. In 1990 it was awarded a contract to plan and install all the heating and ventilation arrangements in a new multi-storey office building commissioned by the Coverite Insurance Company Ltd, who wished to use it for their headquarters. Two engineers, Clarke and Jackson, were assigned to the project. Whilst Clarke was given overall design responsibility, Jackson was detailed off to plan the large central control panel and its associated controls and instrumentation.

Early difficulties

We join the project near the end of the preparation period in the Kosy-Kwik factory. By this time most deliveries of plant and equipment had been made to the Coverite premises, except for the control panel, which was still being fabricated, later than scheduled.

Jackson was a conscientious engineer who took a great interest in his jobs as they passed through the factory. He was in the habit of making periodical tours (management by walking about) to keep a check on progress and the results of his design. During one of these tours the sheet metal shop foreman pointed out to Jackson that the almost-completed control panel was decidedly weak and wobbly.

Jackson could only agree with the foreman. The front panel was indeed decidedly flimsy, as a result of a glaring design error in specifying steel that was far too thin. Delivery of this panel to site was already late, and threatened to delay the whole project. There was simply no time available in which to start making a new control panel. In any case, the extra cost would have been unwelcome. A simpler solution had to be found – a rescue package in fact.

Marked-up drawings

The engineer asked the foreman to weld some suitably chunky pieces of channel iron to the rear face of the panel to stiffen it. The foreman agreed, but was worried about getting the job past the inspection stage with the changes. 'No problem!' said Jackson, who took a pen from his pocket, marked up the foreman's copy of the drawing with the channel iron additions, and signed it to authorize the alteration.

Everyone concerned was very relieved, not least Jackson. Only a few hours were lost, and the stiffened panel was duly delivered to the Coverite plant room. The remainder of the project went ahead without further mishap, and the Coverite Insurance Company Ltd joined the long list of Kosy-Kwik's satisfied customers.

The follow-up project

In the summer of 2000 Kosy-Kwik were awarded a follow-up contract by the Coverite Insurance Company. Coverite's offices were to be extended to house more customer services and staff. Coverite Insurance were working to a well-planned but tight business change schedule, which demanded that the new wing should be opened on the first working day of 2001.

Because of the rigid timescale, Coverite imposed several contract conditions on Kosy-Kwik. In particular, the only complete shut-down period to allow installation and testing the additional circuits and controls was to be during the December 2000 Christmas break. Otherwise the Coverite Company would suffer loss of work by their office staff. Coverite imposed a penalty clause in their contract which would cost Kosy-Kwik £500 for every week or part of a week by which they failed to meet the scheduled end-date.

During the ten years which had separated these two Kosy-Kwik projects several changes had occurred in the Kosy-Kwik organization. Clarke received well-deserved promotion to a remote branch office, where he became area manager. Jackson had retired. The engineering department was bigger, with several new members. Among these was Stevens, an experienced contract engineer. He had no means of contact with Clarke or Jackson, and would never meet either of them.

Preparation for the new project

Stevens was appointed as engineer in charge of the new Coverite project. He knew that the best policy would be to prefabricate as many parts of the project as possible in the factory. This would reduce the amount of work to be done on site, and ensure that the final link-up with the existing system and testing could be done easily during the Christmas break. Stevens found the original Coverite Project drawings in a dead file and set to work.

This system expansion was found to be straightforward, and the final tying-in with the existing installation was to be achieved by providing the installation engineers with a bolt-on package that could be fitted to the original control panel, on which there was plenty of room. This package was duly designed, manufactured and delivered to site along with all the other essential materials. By the time Christmas arrived, all equipment, pipes and ducts were installed in the new part of the building. All that remained was for the final installation team to arrive, shut down the plant, modify the control panel with the kit provided, and then set-up and test the extended system.

The installation attempt

Early on Christmas Eve, two Kosy-Kwik fitters were sent to shut down the plant and start work on the control panel. Their first job was to cut a large rectangular hole in an unused part of the original panel in order to fit the new package. They had been given a template for the hole and placed that in position on the panel. When they started drilling and cutting, the engineers met unexpected resistance in the shape of several large channel iron ribs welded to the rear face of the panel. The engineers had come prepared only to tackle the thin sheet shown on the old drawings. It took them over two hours and many saw blades before the new hole was cut. Then they found that the connections to the new control package were fouled by what remained of the channel iron. Worse still, the panel was now weak and wobbly again.

The two engineers were trained and skilled installation fitters, but were equipped neither materially nor mentally to deal with problems of this magnitude without help. They suffered an acute sense of frustration and isolation, although they found different (much shorter) words with which to express their feelings.

A cry for help back to their Kosy-Kwik headquarters was called for. But this was less than satisfactory. Against the background noise of a lively office party they learned that all the senior engineering and management staff had already left to begin their Christmas holidays. The telephone operator wished the fitters a 'Merry Christmas' and suggested that they 'Have a nice day'. The two engineers interpreted that as good advice, gave up and went home to start their unexpected holidays.

The extra cost

There is no real need to dwell at length on the consequences of this case, or to describe the scenes of anguish and recriminations back at Kosy-Kwik's headquarters in the New Year. A short summary of the additional cost items follows:

		£
1	Design and manufacture new control panel modification kit	3500
2	Cost of time wasted time during first visit of the two fitters	500
3	Cost of repairing weakened panel, on site	180
4	Contract penalty clause, 4 weeks at £400 per week	2000
	Total additional costs, directly attributable	6180

Post-mortem

All Kosy-Kwik's troubles can be traced back to the use of a marked-up drawing in the factory when the earlier project took place. These marked up prints had since been destroyed and the modification had not been incorporated in the filed project drawings.

The use of marked-up drawings is generally to be deplored, but we have to be realistic and accept that there will be occasions when they are unavoidable, when there is not enough time to update the master drawings and reissue them. Under these circumstances, some sort of temporary documentation must suffice, but only where safeguards are in place to ensure that the original drawings do get changed to show the true 'as-built' condition of the project.

If a working copy of a drawing does have to be marked up (which is sometimes unavoidable) an *identical* marked-up copy must be deposited in the design office or attached to a retrospective engineering change request. All this must be done by a suitably senior engineer or designer. When the on-the-spot change has been officially recorded, the original drawing files can be updated in the computer.

12 *Managing Costs*

Many things can happen during the life of a project to alter the expected rate and magnitude of expenditure. The direction of change is usually upwards. Some of the reasons may be unavoidable or unforeseen but, in many cases, the fault will lie somewhere within the project organization. The principal purpose of cost control is to ensure that no preventable wastage of money or unauthorized increase in costs is allowed to happen.

A common misconception is to confuse cost *reporting* with cost *control*. Cost management comprises both reporting and control. Accurate and timely cost reporting is essential, but by itself is not cost control, and perversely, it can add costs to a project without adding any value. By the time overspending is reported, damage has been done. Cost control must be exercised at the time when the costs are being incurred or committed.

A CHECKLIST OF COST MANAGEMENT FACTORS

1. Cost awareness by those responsible for design and engineering.
2. Cost awareness by all other project participants throughout the life of the project.
3. A project work breakdown into packages and tasks of manageable size.
4. Cost budgets, divided so that each work package is given its own share of the total budget.
5. A 'code of accounts' system which can be aligned with the work breakdown structure.
6. A cost accounting system that can collect and analyse costs as they are incurred and allocate them with minimum delay to their relevant cost codes.
7. A practicable work schedule.
8. Effective management of well-motivated staff, to ensure that progress meets or beats the work schedule.
9. A method for comparing expenditure with that planned for the work actually done.
10. Effective supervision and quality control which aims at getting tasks right first time.
11. Proper drafting of specifications and contracts.

12. Discreet investigation to ensure that the customer is of sound financial standing, with sufficient funds available to make all contracted payments.
13. Similar investigation, not necessarily so discreet, of all significant suppliers and subcontractors new to the contractor's experience.
14. Effective use of competitive tendering for all purchases and subcontractors to ensure the lowest costs commensurate with quality and to avoid committing costs that would exceed estimates and budgets.
15. Appropriate consideration and control of modifications and contract variations, including passing justifiable claims for price increases on to the customer.
16. Avoidance, where possible, of unbudgeted dayworks[1] on construction contracts.
17. Where dayworks are unavoidable, proper authorization, retention and administration of dayworks sheets.
18. Strict control of payments to suppliers and subcontractors, to ensure that all invoices and claims for progress payments are neither overpaid nor paid too soon.
19. Recovery from the customer of all incidental expenses allowed for in the contract charging structure (for example, expensive telephone calls, printing, travel and accommodation).
20. Proper invoicing to the customer, especially ensuring that claims for progress payments or cost reimbursement are made at the appropriate times and at the correct levels, so that disputes do not justify the customer delaying payments.
21. Effective credit control to expedite overdue payments from the customer.
22. Occasional internal security audits to prevent losses through theft or fraud.
23. Effective and regular reports of progress and costs to senior management, highlighting potential schedule or budget overruns in time for corrective action to be taken.

Well, with that long list is it surprising that so many projects go over budget?

COST BUDGETS

Project budgets should ideally be derived from the cost estimates used when the tender or internal project proposal (or business case) was prepared. Budgets should set the authorized levels of expenditure for all departments engaged on the project.

Those responsible for checking costs against budgets and progress should be concerned not only with the important top budget limits, but also with the rate at which expenditure is scheduled to take place. When plotted as a graph against time, cumulative project expenditure typically follows an S curve with a slow initial

---

1   Dayworks are small items of work that the customer requests during the course of a construction project. They are too trivial to warrant a contract change variation order, so are typically agreed by the means of orders written on duplicate pads, and signed by authorized representatives of the customer and contractor.

rise, maximum rate of expenditure in the middle period, finally tapering off until the final project cost is reached (see Figure 12.2, for example).

The total budget, minus reserve contingencies, should be allocated over the work breakdown structure so that there is a specified budget for each work package. For true measurement and control, each budget element must correspond to an identifiable and measurable work package. Each of these budget elements and its associated work package needs a unique cost code against which labour timesheet data, material costs and all other direct expenses can be collected and accumulated. Work breakdown and coding was described in Chapter 6.

Labour Budgets

Managers and supervisors should be given their work budgets in terms of man-hours rather than as the resulting costs of wages and overheads. The argument here is that a manager should never be held accountable for meeting targets where they have no authority to control the causal factors. Project managers are rarely directly responsible for wage and salary levels or company overhead expenses. They can, however, be held accountable for the time taken to complete each task.

Budgets for Purchases and Subcontracts

Budgets for purchases and for subcontracts have to be expressed in the appropriate project currency. Relevant packaging, transport, insurance, duties and tax must be included.

Budget Changes

Budgets change (usually upwards) each time a customer-requested change affects the project price. At any time it should be possible for the project budget (and at least the upper level work breakdowns) to be stated in terms of the initial amount, changes subsequently approved, and the combination of these (giving the current total approved budget).

Budget Adjustments for Below-the-line Allowances

If a project lasts more than a few months, cost escalation and (for international projects) foreign exchange fluctuations might have to be taken into account in budgets, cost reporting and control.

Allowances for these below-the-line items can be regarded as 'reserve budgets', provided these were in the original project proposal and have been built into the pricing structure. Appropriate sums can be drawn down from these reserves from time to time to augment the control budget.

Purchased Materials, Equipment and Services

The actual costs of bought-out supplies and services are decided when the purchase orders are issued and accepted by the suppliers (thus creating legal contracts). Purchasing cost control can only be exercised, therefore, when each order is being placed. Once an order has been issued, the costs are usually committed. If the total price agreed exceeds the amount budgeted for the particular item, it is then too late to do anything about it. Any subsequent purchasing cost control procedures can only give early warning of adverse trends.

If purchasing performance was poor, with overspends early in the project, the best that can be done is to ensure that an improvement takes place before the remaining orders are committed.

Graphs of cumulative materials expenditure

A curve can be plotted to show the cumulative value of purchase orders as they are placed. This is a curve of committed expenditure which can be compared with the original budget.

Any curve showing materials commitments will be far more useful if a budget comparison curve is first plotted on the same axes, like a track along which the committed expenditure is expected to run as the points are plotted. The points for plotting the timed budget curve must be calculated by adding together the materials cost estimates for each task, and timing them according to the dates when the orders are scheduled to be issued. Inclusion of milestones on a cost/time graph (as described in the next section) will enhance its value.

MILESTONE ANALYSIS

Milestone analysis is one of the simpler methods managers can use throughout the project life cycle to compare actual costs and progress with the costs and progress planned. The method is less effective than the earned value analysis method described later in this chapter, but it has the merit of needing a relatively modest amount of management effort to set up and maintain. It also requires less sophisticated cost accounting than other methods and can be used when project schedules are not particularly detailed.

Identifying Milestones

Milestones denote particular, easily recognized stages in the progress of a project towards completion. A milestone might be acceptance by the customer of a final design concept, the issue of a package of drawings, the day when a building is made watertight so that internal trades can start, or any other such occasion.

Thus milestone analysis begins by identifying the milestones. Ideally, milestones should coincide with the completion of large packages from the work breakdown structure. That approach will be assumed in the remainder of this discussion. For each milestone, two essential pieces of data are required:

1. The date on which the milestone is scheduled to be achieved.
2. The estimated cost or budget for the associated work package (that is, the expected cost of all the work needed to achieve the milestone).

With all milestone data available, the milestone/budget curve can be plotted. The curve of budgeted expenditure is built up cumulatively, by adding the cost estimates for the work necessary to achieve each milestone, taking care to ensure that the grand project total is equal to the total project cost budget and that no cost estimates are left out.

The date for each milestone is found by reference to the project schedule. Then, with the planned time and cost data available for each milestone, a symbol can be drawn on the budget curve that will show both the planned cost and scheduled date for every milestone in the project.

Plotting the Graph of Actual Expenditure and Milestone Achievement

To be able to plot the graph of actual expenditure for comparison against the plan, two further items of information must be collected. These are:

1. The date on which each milestone was actually achieved.
2. The project costs actually incurred (including committed costs of purchased items) at the end of each cost monitoring period.

It must, therefore, be assumed that a procedure exists for recording the total costs actually incurred or committed for the project at suitable intervals. These intervals might be weekly or monthly, and will depend to some extent on the total life cycle time for the project.

The actual costs can be plotted as a graph on the same axes as the graph of budgeted costs. Points on the graph should be highlighted by symbols to indicate the actual completion date for each milestone. To be able to compare the planned and actual graphs sensibly, each milestone should be identified by a code (simple serial numbers are good for this). If the milestones marked on the budget curve are, for example, numbered 1, 2, 3, 4, and so on, the corresponding points on the actual cost graph can carry the same numbers to make comparison easy.

A Milestone Analysis Example

A construction project expected to last just over one year is the basis for this example. The dotted curve in Figure 12.2 shows the timescaled budget for the project, drawn by combining data from the project schedule and the authorized cost estimates. Thirteen milestones have been identified for the project, and the planned schedule and cost data for these are tabulated in Figure 12.1.

	Milestone description	Schedule (week number)		Cumulative cost £(1000s)	
		Plan	Actual	Budget	Actual
1	Project start authorized	0	6	0	0
2	Design approved	12	14	25	20
3	Drawings issued for building	16	18	60	55
4	Foundations completed	20	22	100	100
5	Drawings issued for services	24	26	180	180
6	All equipment for services ordered	26	28	275	290
7	Walls built to eaves	28	30	345	385
8	Windows and doors finished	32		500	
9	Roof on, building watertight	36		630	
10	Wiring and plumbing finished	40		730	
11	Services installed and tested	44		795	
12	Internal finishes completed	48		825	
13	Site and building handover	56		845	

12.1 Data for a milestone chart

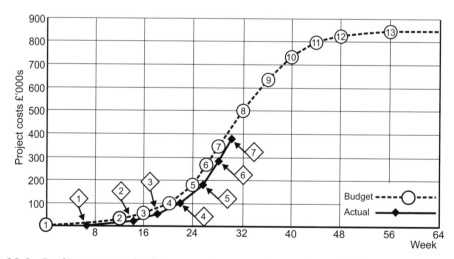

12.2 Project cost and achievement comparison using milestones

Each milestone has been indicated on the planned curve by placing a circle at the time when it should be achieved. The numbers within the circles are codes that identify the milestones.

Monitoring method

Actual cost and progress data have been gathered to the end of week 30 for this project and these are included in Figure 12.1. The results have been plotted, at two-weekly intervals, as the solid line curve in Figure 12.2. Any milestone passed during each two-weekly period has been indicated on the actual cost curve by means of a diamond containing that milestone's identification number.

Interpreting the results

Of course, if all is going exactly according to plan, the budget and actual graphs should lie together on the same path and the milestone points should coincide. When they do not, investigation should give some indication of the project cost and achievement performance to date.

Imagine that you are a senior manager in the company responsible for this project and that it has been running for just over eight weeks. Your project manager has just given you the updated milestone chart. If you look at week 8 (Figure 12.2), you will see that milestone 1, project start, was six weeks late, as indicated by the position of the diamond compared with the circle. The very low costs recorded at week 8 indicate that little or no activity is taking place. So you can easily see that the project has started late and that more effort is needed urgently if progress is to catch up with the plan.

When you receive your updated milestone chart at the end of week 14 it tells you that milestone 2 has now been reached. That should have happened at week 12, but the project has now been pulled up from being six weeks late to only two weeks late. Costs recorded up to week 14 are £25 000. These costs compare with a budget of £20 000 for achieving milestone 2. Expenditure at week 14 should have reached about £45 000 (the dotted budget curve). So you conclude that the project is still running slightly late but the rate of expenditure is lower than plan so that extra effort is needed. You are, however, getting value for the money spent because milestone 2 was achieved for £5000 less than its estimated cost.

If you continue to observe the chart at consecutive two-weekly intervals, you can see how it depicts the changing trend. In particular, the cost performance gradually deteriorates. One significant report from the project manager is the milestone chart updated to the end of week 28. The graphs indicate that milestone 6 should have been achieved at week 26 for a project cost of £275 000. However, milestone 6 has only just been reached at week 28 at a cost of £290 000. So the project is not only still running two weeks late but is also £15 000 over budget.

By week 30, it is apparent that the project programme, as indicated by milestone 7, continues to run two weeks late, and the costs at £385 000 have risen to £40 000 over the corresponding budget for milestone 7.

Without the milestones as measuring points, none of this analysis would have been possible.

Need for replotting

If a change in project scope or any other reason causes rescheduling of work or costs, then the data for future milestones will obviously change too. The curve of predicted expenditure and milestones will have to be amended at each significant authorized change so that it remains up to date and a true basis for comparison of actual costs against plan.

A SIMPLE PERFORMANCE ANALYSIS METHOD FOR DESIGN ENGINEERING

Many projects start their lives in a design department. The easiest approach to assessing design progress is to determine how many drawings and specifications are to be produced, and then divide this number into the number of drawings and specifications actually issued, multiply the answer by one hundred and declare this as the percentage of design completed.

Although I have seen this method used on large projects, it is far too crude because it fails to take into account all the conceptual design work needed and assumes that the work involved in producing one drawing is equivalent to the amount of work needed to produce any other drawing. The method can however be used in limited cases, such as for a department which is producing a large number of similar electrical running diagrams or piping and instrumentation diagrams.

AN OUTLINE OF EARNED VALUE ANALYSIS

Earned value analysis can be regarded as the missing link between cost reporting and cost control. It depends on the existence of a sound framework of planning and control, including the following:

* A detailed work breakdown structure.
* A correspondingly detailed cost coding system.
* Timely and accurate collection and reporting of cost data.
* A method for quantifying the amount of work done, including work in progress.

The earned value process aims to compare the costs incurred for an accurately identified amount of work with the costs budgeted for that work. It can be applied at the level of individual tasks or complete work packages and the data are usually rolled up for the whole project. The procedure uses the results to produce a cost performance index. If everything is going exactly according to plan the cost performance index will be 1.0. An index less than 1.0 indicates that the value earned for the money spent is less than expected, so that the project budget will be overspent.

Earned Value Nomenclature and Definitions

The following are a few of the names and abbreviations used in earned value analysis. The list is not complete but includes the most commonly used quantities.

BCWS   Budgeted cost of work scheduled. This is the budget or cost estimate for work scheduled to be complete at the measurement date. It corresponds with the timescaled budget.

BCWP   Budgeted cost of work performed. This is the amount of money or labour time that the amount of work actually performed at the measurement date should have cost to be in line with the budget or cost estimate. Work in progress should be taken into account in addition to tasks actually completed.

ACWP   Actual cost of the work performed – at the measurement date.

These quantities are used in the following expressions:

$$CPI = \frac{BCWP}{ACWP}$$

$$SPI = \frac{BCWP}{BCWS}$$

where:

CPI   is the cost performance index. This indicates the measure of success in achieving results against budget. Anything less than unity indicates that the value earned from money spent is less than intended.

SPI   is the schedule performance index. This can be used as a measure of progress performance against plan. Anything less than unity shows progress slower than plan. SPI is less commonly used than CPI.

Brick Wall Project: a Very Simple Example of Earned Value Analysis

For this example of earned value analysis I have chosen a project comprising one main activity for which progress can be measured quantitatively without much difficulty or ambiguity.

Imagine a bricklayer and a labourer engaged in building a new boundary wall enclosing a small country estate. If the amount of progress made had to be assessed at any time, work achieved could be measured by the area of wall built or more simply (as here) by the length of wall finished.

The scope, budget and schedule for this project have been defined by the following data:

- Total length of wall to be built = 1000m.
- Estimated total project cost = £40 000.
- Planned duration for the project is 10 weeks (with 5 working days in each week) = 50 days.
- The rate of progress is expected to be steady (linear).

When the above data are considered, the following additional facts emerge:

- Budget cost per day = £800.
- Planned building rate = 20m of wall per day.
- Budget cost for each metre of wall finished = £40.

At the end of day 20 the project manager has been asked to carry out an earned value analysis. The data at the end of day 20 are as follows:

- Work performed: 360 m of wall have been competed.
- ACWP (actual cost of work performed): £18 000. This is the total cost of the task at the end of day 20.
- BCWS (budget cost of work scheduled): 20 days at £800 per day = £16 000.
- BCWP (budget cost of work performed), the 360m of wall actually completed should have cost £40 per metre = £14 400.

Cost implications

The cost implications of these data can be analysed using earned value analysis as follows:

$$\text{The cost performance index (CPI)} = \frac{\text{BCWP}}{\text{ACWP}} = \frac{14\ 400}{18\ 000} = 0.8$$

The implication of this for the final project cost can be viewed in two ways:

1. We could divide the original estimate of £40 000 by the cost performance index and say that the predicted total project cost has risen to £50 000, which gives a projected cost variance of £10 000 for the project.
2. Alternatively, we can say that £18 000 has been spent to date and then work out the likely remaining cost. The 360m of wall built so far have actually cost £18 000, which is a rate of £50 per metre. The amount of work remaining is 640m of wall and, if this should also cost £50 per metre, that will mean a further £32 000 predicted cost remaining to completion. So, adding costs measured to date and remaining costs predicted to completion again gives an estimated total cost at project completion of £50 000.

Schedule implications

Earned value data can also be used to predict the completion date for an activity or a project. The first step is to calculate the schedule performance index. For the wall project at day 20 the SPI is found by:

$$SPI = \frac{BCWP}{BCWS} = \frac{14\ 400}{16\ 000} = 0.9$$

The original estimate for the duration of this project was 50 working days. Dividing by the SPI gives a revised total project duration of about 56 days.

Methods for Assessing the Progress on a Task

Most earned value analysis must be performed not just on one activity (as in the brick wall project just described) but on many project activities. At any time in a large project, three stages of progress can apply to a measured activity. These stages are as follows:

1. Activity not started. Earned value is therefore zero.
2. Activity completed. Earned value is therefore equal to the activity's cost budget.
3. Activity in progress or interrupted. For tasks in construction projects, the earned value can often be assessed by measuring the quantity of work done (as in the brick wall example). For other, less tangible tasks, it is necessary to estimate the proportion or percentage of work done, and then take the same proportion of the current authorized cost estimate as the actual value of work performed.

Earned Value Analysis Reliability

Early predictions of final costs can be unreliable for at least four reasons:

1. Estimates of progress, or of work remaining to completion are subjective judgements, and people usually err on the side of optimism.
2. During the first few weeks or even months of a large project, the sample of work analysed in earned value calculations is too small to produce valid indications of later trends.
3. There is no guarantee that the performance levels early in a project will remain at those same levels throughout the remainder of the project.
4. Additional work might be needed on activities previously reported as complete. For example, drawings and specifications often have to be re-issued with corrections and modifications when they are put to use in manufacturing or construction. Unless due allowance has been made elsewhere for this 'after issue' work, the project budget might eventually be exceeded in spite of earlier favourable predictions from earned value analysis.

What if the Prediction is Bad?

Suppose the actual hours recorded for a project during its progress greatly exceed the earned value expected for that time. The resulting prediction will indicate final costs in well excess of the budget. The first thing to note is that the project manager should be grateful for the early warning. Escape may be possible even from an apparently hopeless situation, provided that suitable action can be taken in time.

Strict control of changes or a design freeze can curb unnecessary expenditure and conserve budgets (although changes requested and paid for by the customer might be welcome because they will add to the budget). Unfunded changes should be only be allowed if they are essential for project safety, reliability and performance.

In the face of vanishing budgets, the demands made on individuals will have to be more stringent. But this can be helped through good communications, by letting all the participants know what the position is, what is expected of them and why. It is important to gain their full cooperation. The project manager will find this easiest to achieve within a project team organization. If the organization is a matrix, the project manager must work through all the departmental managers involved to achieve the essential good communications and motivation.

People's performance can often be improved by setting short- and medium-term objectives, but these must always be fair and feasible. Targets should be expressed in measurable quantities (for example time or money) so that assessment can be fair and objective. Individuals should be encouraged to monitor their own performance. These personal objectives should equate with the project objectives of time, cost and performance through the work breakdown structure. When work is done on time, it is far more likely that the cost objective will be met.

If, in spite of all efforts, a serious overspend still threatens, there remains the possibility of replenishing the project coffers from their original source – the customer. This feat can sometimes be accomplished by re-opening a fixed-price negotiation whenever a suitable opportunity presents itself. An excuse to renegotiate may be provided, for example, if the customer should ask for a substantial change, or as a result of external economic factors that are beyond the contractor's control. Failing these steps, smaller modifications or project spares can be priced generously to help offset the areas of loss or low profitability. Care must also be taken to invoice the customer for every item that the contract allows to be charged as a project expense.

Remember that without earned value analysis, forewarning of possible overspending may not be received in time to allow any corrective action at all. The project manager must always be examining cost trends, rather than historical cost reports.

When the predictions are bad, despair is the wrong philosophy. It is far better to reappraise the remaining project activities and explore all possible avenues that could restore the original project targets.

EFFECT OF CHANGES ON EARNED VALUE ANALYSIS

Every modification or change introduced into a project can be expected to have some effect on the measured level of achievement attained by the departments involved. Before this effect can be considered for any particular change, one significant question must always be answered:

* Can the customer be held liable for any additional costs, or must the additional work be paid for out of the existing budget (and, therefore, out of the potential profits)?

Control of changes was discussed in the previous chapter. It can be assumed that long before any change is implemented, the change committee or other designated authority will have ensured that the change is clearly defined as 'unfunded' or 'customer-funded'.

Unfunded Changes

Each unfunded change will usually increase the workload remaining with no corresponding increase in the authorized budgets. That will depress the earned value proportion measured in all the departments affected.

It would be possible to make an appropriate correction for unfunded changes to the achievement measurement for each department. Each change would have to be added to the task list, along with a cost estimate for the additional work needed. There can, of course, be no corresponding increase in the authorized budget.

In practice (although I have been criticized in the past for taking this approach) such adjustments are unnecessary, and unfunded changes can be ignored provided that:

- they are not too numerous or horrendous; and
- they do not cancel out work already reported as achieved.

The costs of modifications or project changes are extremely difficult to estimate and record, because of the way in which the work is intermingled with the original tasks affected. If, for instance, a wiring diagram is changed for a complex piece of equipment, it can be impossible to work out the changed cost of carrying out the wiring, especially if the task happened to be in progress at the time of the change.

Unfunded changes will therefore appear as overspending, which is of course just what they really are. Achievement predictions will be self-correcting as these overspends are picked up.

Completed work scrapped by unfunded changes

Unfunded changes that nullify work already carried out must always be taken into account by erasure of the relevant achievement from the records. This should be done for every department affected, and either whole tasks or parts of them may have to be reinstated into the remaining workload.

Customer-funded Changes

Funded changes can be considered as new tasks, for addition both to the task list and its authorized budgets. The customer should be asked to pay for work which is scrapped as a result of the modification, in which case that work can be considered as having been sold and, therefore, achieved. It need not be subtracted from the achievement tally.

THE PROJECT LEDGER CONCEPT

A picture has now been built up of a collection of methods by which data can be displayed on graphs or in tables to show the predicted and measured performance against plans and budgets. Although space only allowed a simple brick wall project to be demonstrated, the procedures for departments and operations in far more complex projects follow the same principles.

Successful budgetary control and cost prediction require some accurate bookkeeping, not only within the accounts department, but also under the administration of the project manager. The resulting dossier of achievement returns, estimates and budgets, all collated with respect to the project WBS, can be regarded as a project ledger.

The ledger is credited with the initial cost budgets plus any authorized additions, such as those arising from customer-requested changes (variation orders, for instance).

The value of work achieved, expressed in cost terms, is debited from the ledger as it is reported.

A balance is left outstanding which represents the estimated cost of work remaining. It should always be possible to consult the ledger to determine the current cost/budget/achievement status of every department engaged on the project.

The ledger will probably be set up in a computer, either in a central management information system or using one of the more powerful project management packages. The method requires considerable effort and is not easy to apply successfully because of the difficulty in obtaining and maintaining accurate data.

PREDICTING PROFITABILITY FOR A PROJECT

When earned value calculations can be collected from all parts of the project organization, it is a logical and progressive step to pool the results and predict the final project costs.

Of course, the first such prediction is made before the start of the project, when the initial cost estimates and budgets are prepared and when progress can confidently be declared as zero. Subsequent analysis and cost prediction can be regarded as a continuous process by which the original estimate is steadily refined. As more work is completed, the estimate of costs remaining to completion contains an increasing proportion of actual cost data, so that the predictions should become more accurate.

For cost control, data must be presented in a way that shows unwanted trends as early as possible, before it becomes too late for anything to be done. Graphical methods can be used but a tabulation or spreadsheet can show more detail. Spreadsheets can be read more easily and accurately, without the scaling errors common to graphs.

Spreadsheet Presentation

Project cost summaries and predictions are commonly presented in tabular or spreadsheet form. Figure 12.3 shows a widely used arrangement, suitable for preparation from clerical methods or from computer systems. Tables such as this are typically bound into regular cost and progress reports, often produced at monthly intervals.

Column A lists project tasks. In a very tiny project, this might be a task list but for any project of significant size it would list the first level items from the work breakdown structure. The listing in column A must include all cost items, including software tasks and summarized miscellaneous items. Back-up sheets are usually needed, assembled in sets showing more detail and arranged in a logical structure (usually the hierarchical work breakdown).

Column B lists the cost code of every main project section. This makes it easier to refer back to the original estimates and budgets, to audit the data presented and to process the data in a computer.

In column C the original budgets for the tasks are shown, and these should add up to the total authorized cost budget, derived from the original project cost estimates. Consideration must be given to the inclusion or otherwise of escalation and other below-the-line estimates, and it may be necessary to add explanatory notes in the accompanying report text.

As the project proceeds, it can be expected that a number of variations or modifications will arise that are agreed with the client, and for which the client will pay. These will increase both the project revenue and the budget. Budget increments from this cause are listed in column D. These, when added to the original budget for each project section, give the current revised authorized budgets, shown in column E.

A	B	C	D	E	F	G	H	J	K	L
Item	Cost code	Original budget	Authorized budget changes	Authorized current budget	ACWP	BCWP (assessed)	CPI	Forecast costs remaining (E-G)/H	Forecast costs at completion F+J	Forecast variance at completion E-K

Project cost report summary — Page of — Project title: — Project number: — Report date:

12.3 A project cost report that shows predictions based on earned value analysis

In any project of significant size there are usually variations under consideration or awaiting approval that could ultimately affect the budget (and progress assessment). Until such variations have been agreed with the client it is not possible to take the additional revenue for granted. It may, nevertheless, be of considerable interest to know the value of any such proposals which happen to be 'in the pipeline' at the report date. Some people include a column in their report formats to show the costs of these pending variations. This has not been done here owing to limited space.

Column F lists the costs actually recorded up to and including the report date. In earned value analysis terms these are the actual costs of work performed (ACWP). They comprise the following:

1. Direct labour hours booked to the project (on timesheets or job tickets) converted at standard cost or other appropriate rates into the project control currency.
2. A pro rata allowance to cover overheads and administrative costs.
3. Payments for directly relevant insurance premiums, licences, legal fees and consultants' fees.
4. Payments made to, or legitimately claimed by, subcontractors.
5. The cost of all materials committed, which includes the cost of materials and equipment already used or delivered, plus the value of all other materials and equipment for which orders have been placed at the report date. In all cases freight, packing, insurance, agents' fees and duties paid or committed must be included.
6. Any other costs incurred or committed up to the report date that can be directly attributed to the project.

Column G in Figure 12.3 is the budgeted cost of work actually performed (BCWP). This is the best possible judgement of earned value that can be made, taking care to include allowances for work-in-progress as well as for tasks actually completed.

Column H shows the cost performance index (CPI), the factor derived from comparing the figures in columns F and G. This factor is applied to the original budget for the work remaining to predict the likely remaining project cost (in column J).

Adding the forecast remaining costs to the actual expenditure to date yields the best possible estimate of what the project final total cost will be (column K). As time passes, the forecast element of this figure will become less, the proportion of actual costs will become greater, and the final prediction will grow more accurate.

The final column, L, in Figure 12.3 shows the expected difference (variance) between the final project costs and the approved budget.

MANAGING CASH FLOW

Cash is the lifeblood of businesses and their projects. Without money to pay the people, suppliers and subcontractors, all work must stop and even the most promising project will fail.

The subject of project cash flow is often misunderstood. Two common mistakes are:

1. confusing cash *outflow* schedules with *net* cash flow schedules;
2. regarding a predicted final project profit and loss statement as being completely satisfactory if it forecasts a good end result, but giving no thought to the cash flows that must take place before the project can be finished.

The easiest way to appreciate cash flow management is to imagine yourself as the project contractor, and picture the cash payments flowing into and out of the project as if they were flowing in and out of your personal bank balance. Thus you must manage cash inflows and outflows so that the account does not go into an unauthorized level of borrowing.

Cash flow management means getting all payments into the project on or very soon after their due dates. These typically include stage payments (progress payments) that are linked to project milestones or invoices certified by an independent authority to prove that the amount of work claimed for has, in fact been done. If a project runs late, such payments cannot be claimed from the customer, and cash flow difficulties might result.

Credit control is important. That means ensuring that customers are not allowed to default on legitimate claims for payment.

The project manager might be asked to advise the financial department of predicted cash requirements by preparing a cash flow schedule before the project begins. That means going through a series of logical steps, as shown in Figure 12.4. Note how often that word 'logical' appears in project management! Figure 12.5 is an example to show how a cash flow schedule should be laid out in spreadsheet style.

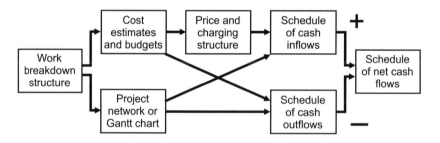

12.4 Logical steps required to calculate a net cash flow schedule

Main contractors and other managers of large capital projects may be asked to predict cash flows as a service to their clients. Those clients need to know when to expect claims for payment from the contractor. In some very large capital projects, customers set up accounts from which to pay for project equipment themselves, relying on advice from the main project contractor for release of instructions to pay. This is another case where clients need to be advised in advance of the likely amounts and timings of their commitments.

So project cash flow schedules can serve a dual purpose, helping both the contractor and the customer to make the necessary funds available to keep the project afloat and financially viable.

PROJECTS UNLIMITED LTD — Loxylene Chemical Plant for Lox Chemical Company

Project number P21900
Issue date March 2012

Quarterly periods – all figures £1,000s

Cost item	2013				2014				2015				2016				2017	Total budget
	1	2	3	4	1	2	3	4	1	2	3	4	1	2	3	4	1	
INFLOWS																		
Agreed loans	50				150													200
Client's payments	10		50	100	200	500	1500	1000	1000	1750	1000	1000	1000	3000	1000	1000	1000	15110
Total inflows	60		50	100	350	500	1500	1000	1000	1750	1000	1000	1000	3000	1000	1000	1000	15310
OUTFLOWS																		
Engineering	14	25	59	80	85	63	43	23	12	11	9	6	7	10	14	14		475
Purchasing		5	45	5	550	310	745	295	750	665	215	457	2242	76	2	470		6832
Construction				17	35	97	245	393	436	654	382	241	186	45	30			2761
Contingency					10	20	25	25	30	30	35	35	45	45	50	50		400
Escalation					35	29	74	59	110	136	70	88	322	30	32	85		1070
Total outflows	14	30	104	102	715	519	1132	795	1338	1496	711	827	2802	206	128	619		11538
NET FLOWS																		
Periodic	46	(30)	(54)	(2)	(365)	(19)	368	205	(338)	254	289	173	(1802)	2794	872	381	1000	
Cumulative	46	16	(38)	(40)	(405)	(424)	(56)	149	(189)	65	354	527	(1275)	1519	2391	2772	3772	3772

12.5 Net cash flow schedule for a construction project

CLOSING THE PROJECT DOWN

Just as it was necessary to issue a formal document of authority to open a project and allow expenditure to begin, so the end of a project or its indefinite interruption must be marked by a formal announcement that stops further expenditure and sets the closure procedures in motion.

Cost Cut-off

The most significant reason for issuing a formal project closure statement is to forbid further expenditure against the main project cost accounts. This is particularly important if hard-won profits are not to be eroded by an insidious continuation of timesheet bookings to the project simply because the account still happens to be open. It is well known that the recording of hours on timesheets is open to abuse; there is always a tendency for the less scrupulous staff to try and 'lose' unaccountable or wasted time by booking it to large projects where, it is hoped, it will go unnoticed. Good supervision and timesheet audits will minimize this risk, but an instruction to the computer to reject all further timesheet entries against the project number is more effective.

Company accountants may wish to hold a project account open for their own use beyond the official project closure date to collect a few tail-end costs. There are usually items such as late invoices from suppliers and subcontractors to be accounted for. On a large project these can continue to arrive for several months after project completion. They can represent considerable sums, but they should not affect the calculated profit significantly because (unless there has been loose control of subcontracts and dayworks) these costs should have been known and accrued in the accounts when they were committed (that is, when the purchase orders or subcontracts were issued).

Project Closure Document

The formal closure notice need only be a very simple form, but it should contain the following information:

- project title
- project number
- the effective closure date
- reason for closure
- any special instructions
- signature authorizing the closure
- distribution, which should at least include all those who received the authorization notice when the project was opened.

Notice of project closure							
The following project will be closed to time bookings and all expenses with effect from the date given below							
Client: **Lox Chemicals Limited**					Project number: **LX 5150**		
Project title: **Loxylene Plant (Huddersfield)**					Closure date: **20 Apr 12**		
The following budgets are hereby authorized for the closedown activities marked in the checklist below							
Department	hours by standard cost staff grade						£
	1	2	3	4	5	6	
Project engineering	10			20	40		960
Planning				10			140
Purchasing			15				240
Installation and commissioning							
Construction management	5						100
Computing				1			14
Records and archives			10		200		2560
TOTALS	15		25	31	240		4014

Special instructions:

    Take special care with filing. A follow-up project is expected. All files to be destroyed after six years unless otherwise directed below.

CHECKLIST OF PROJECT CLOSURE ACTIVITIES	
Project case history	PM to write, keep it brief
Project specification	Has been kept up to date but needs checking
Project variations	List and check that the file is complete
Drawing schedules	Keep 10 years in engineering files
Design calculations	Keep indefinitely in engineering files
Our drawings	Check they are as-built and keep indefinitely
Client's drawings	Return to client
Purchase control schedules	Keep 10 years in engineering files
Vendors' drawings	Keep 10 years
Purchase orders	
Expediting/inspection reports	
Test certificates	Keep 10 years
Operating/maintenance instructions	Keep 15 years
Spares lists	
Maintenance contracts	
Subcontract documents	Keep 10 years
Correspondence files	
Final cost records	Keep 10 years in general reference files
Photographs	Edit. Discuss with publicity dept and client
Critical path networks	Destroy after 1 year and erase computer files
Management information system	Delete project from MIS at year end

Prepared by: **A.Scribe**   Project manager: **I.Diddit**   Authorized by: *B. I. G. Whitechief*

12.6 Project closure notice with checklist

An example of a fairly comprehensive closure notice from a company in my past experience is given in Figure 12.6. This version contains a checklist of possible closure tasks.

Post-mortem

When the project is finished and the final costs become known an investigation can be conducted to compare the actual expenditure with the original estimates. Such post-mortem examinations are far too late to be of benefit to the completed project, but they can be helpful in identifying errors in design and management to be avoided when estimating or conducting future projects. When time and money allow, some contractors ask the project manager to compile a concise project diary to record the most significant events and experiences.

13 Corporate Managers' Support for the Project Manager

Imagine that you are a senior manager or director of a company that carries out projects. Indeed you might be such a manager. This chapter is written as an open letter to you. For the most part it doesn't matter here what kind of projects your company is involved with.

If you have never managed a project yourself you will not know, and may never need to know, the day-to-day things that your project managers do at their tactical level. Of course that is not important. You delegate all those details and must rely on your subordinates. But, you do have to be aware that strategic decisions made by you and your fellow senior managers can, at one extreme, create conditions that help your project managers to do their jobs very well. At the other extreme, neglect or bad strategic decisions can make their working lives impossible, so that your projects will fail and your company, your clients, and all the other stakeholders will suffer.

COSTS AND BENEFITS OF PROJECT MANAGEMENT

Project Management as a Cost Burden

Unless you manage a company (such as a managing contractor) that sells project management as a service, or you can otherwise sell your project managers' time to your clients as a direct project cost, you know that every project manager you employ will add another salary to your overheads. Further, each will occupy space and use other company facilities that also have to be paid for. Then, apparently, it gets even worse than that, because project managers need help from support staff, so adding still more indirect salaries and expenses. So, at first glance, project management is not free. It comes at a cost. And an indirect cost, at that.

Benefits

Every project that is finished on time will stand a far greater chance of being delivered within or below budget costs. Indeed, far from adding costs to a project, a mix of a good project management and common sense can typically knock as much as 30 per cent off the direct costs of a project (when compared with similar projects conducted by the same company in the past without competent project management). Now *that* is a good return on investment.

All projects have their risks and crises, but where there is good project management those episodes are minimized. Indeed, risk forecasting and assessment is a valuable part of the duties of many project support offices. When a project is running smoothly, its technical staff spend less of their effort in fighting fires and have more time to concentrate on delivering quality. Project management therefore facilitates completion within specification.

Efficient management of any project carried in-house is equally important but, unlike projects delivered to an external customer or client, the expectations for internal projects extend beyond completion of the initial project. For these projects there is almost always a vital implementation period, during which the project manager and all other company managers must be committed to the project and its success if the full benefits are to be realized for the company.

A company that achieves success with its projects, whether these are in-house or for external clients, can expect to gain benefits beyond those predicted for the project itself. When project management creates orderly working, without the problems of materials shortages, resource overloads, late deliveries and so on, you as a senior manager will find that your cash flow should improve, because deliveries on time mean you can call your revenues in on time. For industrial projects, your inventory turn rate should improve because work in progress will take less time and so reduce in volume.

Success spreads happiness and contentment. If project management creates a working environment where the stresses of day-to-day panics are removed, that relief of stress should permeate the whole company as people become more relaxed at work. These are not just weasel words. This is written from personal experience.

Getting Value for the Cost of Project Management

Some project management functions are essential, others are desirable, and still others fall into the nice-to-have but not really necessary category. Of course every facet of project management has its dedicated advocates, but some project management activities are more necessary than others.

Much will depend on how much information you (as a senior manager) and your clients want, because compiling and reporting information for a large project can be expensive. There is much to be said for the principle of *management by exception* – which from your position as a senior manager means you should expect your project manager to report to you in detail only the things that are not running to plan or which otherwise might give cause for concern. That is often difficult to accept. You like to see well-produced graphs and pie charts showing that your projects are running to plan and budget. But those reports might cost more money to produce than you realize. And more costs in this instance usually translates to additional staff in the project support office. It is not always obvious what functions are vital to efficient project management and which functions are simply nice to have.

Functions essential to project management

A project is a living thing and like all living things it needs a parent or someone to 'own' it, to care for it from birth to maturity. So we must have project managers. Not necessarily one for each project, because there are cases where one project manager can oversee two or more small projects.

Now, as a senior manager, you have every right to question who else needs to work in the project office. You will want to justify every overhead salary.

Every project needs a schedule and detailed budgets if it is to be controlled, and those in turn require initial work breakdowns and cost estimates. Thus projects need planners and cost engineers, although for a very small project it is possible that a multi-skilled project manager can carry out these functions without assistance. For larger projects you must have at least one planner and one cost engineer, and they will form the nucleus of your project management office (PMO).

If your typical project is a large one for a paying client, you can be certain that variation orders or other changes will happen. Each of those variations, although probably a nuisance, can bring in valuable additional revenue. Indeed some companies claim that they bid for their projects using a very low mark-up on prime costs and expect to make their profits by charging as much as possible for the inevitable crop of contract variations caused by the client. As each project proceeds your company will need to keep track of those changes so that you do not lose the chance to recover all those additional and valuable revenues. So day-to-day contract administration is needed, and that can be part of the project support office's role. It does not always need a full-time appointment. The function only becomes difficult and very expensive when changes on a large contract are allowed to go unrecorded, so that a horrible clean-up operation has to take place before final invoicing can be agreed after project completion.

Project 'management' functions that do not manage the project

For statutory accounting purposes, for example when compiling tax returns or preparing company accounts, it is clearly necessary to record the costs of labour and purchases. So the accounts department has to analyse timesheets and run its payroll, bought ledgers and invoice control functions. But many projects have their own additional accounting functions, usually in a project support office, to attempt to compare costs and progress. One form of this is seen in earned value 'management'.

But consider this. Cost *reporting* is not cost *control*. That begs the question, 'What is cost control'.

From the project management point of view, the direct costs of a project (assuming that all the design people are competent) are controlled by:

- Having good project definition in the first place;
- Avoiding changes not requested by a paying customer;
- Efficient purchasing and materials management (remembering that the cost of bought materials and services is as high as 80 per cent of the total cost of some projects);
- Keeping work on progress against a practical schedule – because work that runs late will invariably overrun budget.

These, really, are the most important factors in the control of direct costs. Of course many other things can improve the performance of people working on the project and many of those things are subjects for other chapters in this book.

Earned value management for a large project can be a very difficult operation to get right and can consume many hours. It might be unavoidable, for example when it is used to evaluate progress payments invoiced to a client, and that clearly impacts on credit control and cash flow. But it is nonetheless an overhead cost that adds no value to the project. It should really be called earned value *measurement*. It does have a role in assessing performance early in the project so that undesirable trends can be identified and corrected, but measurements early in a project tend to be inaccurate because they are based on insufficient data.

Your clients might expect regular cost and progress reports and, if they do, they must be given them. But remember that every time you, as a senior corporate manager, ask one of your project managers for anything other than a simple cost report from your accountants, someone in the project support office will have to prepare that report and your company, not the project client, will have to bear the report preparation cost. If you were to investigate the amount of effort needed to support investigative cost reports (such as earned value reports) you would probably be astounded, because that effort involves all the managers and supervisors working on the project – the final reports are a roll-up of all their individual reports.

So, although this chapter is really a plea for you, as a corporate manager, to support your project managers, it is right that some costs should be questioned before you sanction them.

ACTIVE SUPPORT FROM SENIOR MANAGEMENT FOR PROJECT MANAGEMENT

Project managers need support in various forms from their superiors. This section discusses some of the ways in which you, as a senior manager, can help to ensure that your project management function operates efficiently and without avoidable stress.

A Project Room

Every project manager needs access to a room where project meetings can be held. If possible a room (which does not have to be expensively decorated and fitted out) should be available that the project manager can use as a project 'war room', where plans and drawings can be pinned to walls and where ad hoc meetings of small groups or others can take place informally without ceremony to discuss project matters. Such a room can help the project to have its own identity. It can also help to create a team spirit where no team actually exists in the organization (such as in a matrix organization, as described in Chapter 10).

A secure project room, that can be kept locked when project staff are not in attendance, is valuable for projects that have to be carried out in an atmosphere of secrecy or confidentiality. That might be required in circumstances where client confidentiality has to be preserved, for management change projects where early leakage of the work could lead to the spread of unsettling rumours, or for work carried out under The Official Secrets Act (or its equivalent in countries other than the UK).

Software and Computing Equipment

Projects benefit from the use of purpose-designed software such as Primavera, Deltek's Open Plan, and so on. Your project manager should be the best judge of which software to use. That might result in conflict with your IT manager (it happened to me once and resulted in enmity over a long period). As a senior manager you should generally support the project manager's choice, However, if you have more than one project and more than one project manager, you must ensure that they all agree on one common system – or at least on systems that are mutually compatible. Otherwise difficulties will arise, especially if multi-project scheduling across all your projects is required.

The purchase of project management software is a big investment, not particularly in terms of money, but because of the effort needed to set up the project records and maintain them. If the choice of software is wrong, the remedy can be painful and expensive. So, please take a sympathetic but careful interest in any request from a project manager for the purchase of project management software.

Providing an Appropriate Project Organization

The organizational structure of your company and its projects can greatly affect the way in which people in projects work and communicate. Organization structures are discussed in Chapter 5, and that chapter should be of interest to senior managers like yourself, because organization design is a strategic function for senior management. Project managers do not often enjoy the luxury of choosing or changing the organization in which they are expected to work. It is usual for project managers to be appointed to project organizations that already exist and which have been established by others beyond their control – by you or your fellow senior managers. So you can help and support your project managers by listening to any difficulties they might experience that are a direct result of the organization and communications structure in which you have placed them.

Sometimes restructuring an organization can improve communications and motivation of all those working on projects beyond measure. However, organizational change can be disruptive to work in progress, so you will have to decide on the best timing.

It might be that the organization pattern can be left undisturbed but you will have to change or define more specifically the relative authority and balance of power between the project managers and your functional managers. That balance of power can be a particular difficulty in matrix organizations.

Only you or other senior managers can implement such organizational changes – your project managers do not have that power and they must rely on your support.

Training

Project management is still an evolving profession. Qualified project managers will be expected by their professional associations to maintain current awareness of techniques and working practices. Project managers enhance their value to your company by continuous learning, and by attending meetings where they can share experiences and learn from their peers and more senior practitioners.

Many of these meetings take place out of office hours, in your project manager's leisure time. But occasionally important seminars and international congresses are arranged by the professional project management associations and you should give sympathetic consideration to supporting time off and travel, at least for your more senior and most successful project managers.

Personal Support and Encouragement

Kerzner (2000) conducted a survey of some 600 American companies to investigate the process of project management implementation. Many people responded to questionnaires issued by Professor Kerzner. The results make fascinating reading. One case remains especially fixed in my mind. A very talented and competent woman spent years of her life creating an enthusiastic project management culture in the company that employed her, and everyone was benefiting from her work and inspiration. All was blown away when the company underwent several senior management changes and corporate support was withdrawn (ibid., pp. 111–114). Kerzner concluded: 'Executive project sponsorship must exist and be visible so that the project-line manager interface is in balance'.

But executive 'sponsorship and support' can be as simple as occasionally visiting project people at their workplaces, taking an interest in what they do, and giving praise when a project is successful. Such praise and encouragement costs nothing. The return on this zero investment can be very valuable.

REFERENCE

Kerzner, H. (2000), *Applied Project Management: Best Practices on Implementation*, New York, Wiley.

Select Bibliography

APM Earned Value Specific Interest Group (2002), *Earned Value Management: APM Guide for the UK*, High Wycombe, APM.

APM (2012), *APM Body of Knowledge*, 6th edn, Princes Risborough, Association for Project Management.

Basu, R. (2011), *Managing Project Supply Chains*, Farnham, Gower.

Belbin, R.M. (2010), *Management Teams: Why They Succeed or Fail*, 3rd edn, Oxford, Butterworth-Heinemann.

Bradley, G. (2010), *Benefit Realisation Management: A Practical Guide to Achieving Benefits Through Change*, 2nd edn, Farnham, Gower.

Buchanan, D.A. and Huczyinski, A. (2010), *Organizational Behaviour*, 7th edn, Harlow, Pearson Education.

Buttrick, R. (2005), *The Project Workout*, 3rd edn, London, FT Prentice Hall.

Carroll, T. (2006), *Project Delivery in Business-as-Usual Organizations*, Aldershot, Gower.

Chapman, R.J. (2014), *The Rules of Project Risk Management: Implementation Guidelines for Major Projects*, Farnham, Gower.

Devaux, S.A. (1999), *Total Project Control: a Manager's Guide to Integrated Planning, Measuring and Tracking*, New York, Wiley.

Eskerod, P. and Jepsen, A.L. (2012), *Project Stakeholder Management*, Farnham, Gower.

Fleming, Q.W. and Koppelman, J.M. (2010), *Earned Value Project Management*, 4th edn, Newtown Square, PA, Project Management Institute.

Gattorna, J.L. (ed.) (2003), *Gower Handbook of Supply Chain Management*, 5th edn, Aldershot, Gower.

Goldsmith, L. (2005), *Project Management Accounting: Budgeting, Tracking, and Reporting Costs and Profitability*, Chichester, Wiley.

Gordon, J. and Lockyer, K. (2005), *Project Management and Project Planning*, 7th edn, London, FT Prentice Hall.

Gray, B., Gray, C.F. and Larson, E.W. (2010), *Project Management: the Managerial Process*, 5th edn, Singapore, McGraw-Hill.

Harrison, F. and Lock, D. (2004), *Advanced Project Management: A Structured Approach*, 4th edn, Aldershot, Gower.

Hartman, F.T. (2000), *Don't Park Your Brain Outside*, Newtown Square, PA, Project Management Institute.

Hillson, D. (2009), *Managing Risk in Projects*, Farnham, Gower.

Hulett, D. (2009), *Practical Schedule Risk Analysis*, Farnham, Gower.

Hulett, D. (2011), *Integrated Cost-Schedule Risk Analysis* (companion to the above book), Farnham, Gower.

Kerzner, H. (2000), *Applied Project Management: Best Practices on Implementation*, New York, Wiley.

Kerzner, H. (2011), *Project Management: A Systems Approach to Planning, Scheduling and Controlling*, 11th edn, Hoboken, NJ, Wiley.

Lester, A. (2006), *Project Planning and Control*, 5th edn, Oxford, Butterworth-Heinemann.

Lock, D. (2004), *Project Management in Construction*, Aldershot, Gower.

Lock, D. (2013), *Naked Project Management: The Bare Facts*, Farnham, Gower.

Lock, D. (2013), *Project Management*, 10th edn, Farnham, Gower.

Lock, D and Scott, L. (2013), *The Gower Handbook of People in Project Management*, Farnham, Gower.

Mantel, S.J., Meredith, J.R., Shafer, S.M. and Sutton, M.M. (2011), *Project Management in Practice*, 4th edn, New York, Wiley.

Marsh, D.E. (2000), *The Project and Programme Support Office*, vol 1 (Foundation), Hook, Project Manager Today.

Marsh, D.E. (2000), *The Project and Programme Support Office*, vol 2, (Advanced), Hook, Project Manager Today.

Maylor, H. (210), *Project Management*, 4th edn, London, FT Prentice Hall.

Meredith, J.R. and Mantel, S.J. Jnr (2003), *Project Management: a Managerial Approach*, 5th edn, New York, Wiley.

Morris, P. (1994), *The Management of Projects*, London, Thomas Telford.

Nalewaik, A. (2013), *Project Cost Recording and Reporting*, Farnham, Gower.

Nicholas, J.M. and Steyn, J.H. (2012), *Project Management for Engineering, Business and Technology*, 4th edn, Abingdon, Routledge.

Office of Government Commerce (2009), *Managing Successful Projects with PRINCE2*, London, OGC.

PMI (2013), *A Guide to the Project Management Body of Knowledge (PMBOK® Guide)*, 5th edn, Newtown Square, PA, Project Management Institute.

Rodrigues, A. (2013), *Earned Value Management for Programmes and Portfolios*, Farnham, Gower.

Rodrigues, A. (2013), *Earned Value Management for Projects*, Farnham, Gower.

Rosenau, M.D. Jnr and Githens, G.D. (2005), *Successful Project Management: A Step-by-Step Approach with Practical Examples*, 4th edn, Wiley, New York.

Sadgrove, K. (2005), *The Complete Guide to Business Risk Management*, 2nd edn, Aldershot, Gower.

Salkeld, D. (2013), *Project Risk Analysis*, Farnham, Gower.

Slack, N., Chambers, S. and Johnston, R. (2007), *Operations Management*, 5th edn, Harlow, FT Prentice Hall.

Stuzke, R.D. (2005), *Software Project Estimation, Projects, Products and Processes*, Boston, MA, Addison Wesley.

Taylor, P. (2009), *The Lazy Project Manager: How to be Twice as Productive and Still Leave the Office Early*, Oxford, Infinite Ideas.

Taylor, P. (2011), *Leading Successful PMOs: How to Build the Best Project Management Office for Your Business*, Farnham, Gower.

Turner, J.R. (ed.) (2014), *Gower Handbook of Project Management*, 5th edn, Aldershot, Gower.

Turner, J.R. (ed.) (2003), *Contracting for Project Management*, Aldershot, Gower.

Ward, G. (2008), *Project Manager's Guide to Purchasing*, Aldershot, Gower.

Webb, A. (2000), *Project Management for Successful Product Innovation*, Aldershot, Gower.

Webb, A. (2003), *Using Earned Value: A Project Manager's Guide*, Aldershot, Gower.

Webb, A. (2003), *The Project Manager's Guide to Handling Risk*, Aldershot, Gower.

Wren, A. (2003), *The Project Management A-Z: A Compendium of Project Management Techniques and How to Use Them*, Aldershot, Gower.

Wright, D. (2004), *Law for Project Managers*, Aldershot, Gower.

Index

4c Systems 116, 119

Achievement measurement *see*
      Earned value analysis
Activity-on-arrow networks *see*
      Arrow diagrams (ADM) *under*
      Critical path networks
Activity-on-node networks *see*
      Precedence diagrams (PDM)
      under Critical path networks
Actual cost of work performed
      (ACWP) 181–2, 188–9
After-issue work 40
Arrow diagrams (ADM) *see*
      Critical path networks
Artemis 116
As-built condition 15, 170
Association for Project
      Management (APM) 12

Ballpark cost estimates 31
Bar charts 83–7, 94–5, 108–9,
      112–13, 116–17, 131
   as progress monitoring aids 26
   furniture project example 84–6
   limitations of 94
   linked 85, 94
Below-the-line costs 30,175, 188
Benefits realization 11–12, 17
Best, enemy of the good 26
Bid summaries 147, 149

Bikes 'n' Skates project case
      example 23–6
Brick wall project case example 182–3
Budget cost of work performed
      (BCWP) 181–3, 188–9
Budget cost of work scheduled
      (BCWS) 181–3
Budgets 3, 5, 7–8, 16, 23, 26, 29–31,
      33, 35, 37–8, 72–3, 78, 80,
      87, 116–17, 120–21, 124,
      150, 154–5, 173–91, 196–8
Business change projects *see*
      Management change and IT
      projects

Calendars 95, 107–9
Cash flow 99, 189–91, 196, 198
Certificates for payments 8,
      61, 152, 155, 190
Change committee (or change
      board) 161–2, 165, 167, 185
Changes and modifications
   authorization 160–62
   classification 160
   commercial (contract)
      administration 164–5, 197
   contract variation orders 163–4
   coordinating clerk 162
   decision criteria 161–2
   design freeze 167
   emergency modifications 167–71

engineering change
    requests 165–6, 171
impact in relation to the
    project life cycle 159–62
interchangeability rule 167
marked up drawings 168, 170
procedures and forms 163–6
project variation orders 163–3
registration 162
Checklists
    construction projects 18
    cost management factors 173–4
    mining project 19
    project closure 193–4
    project definition 128
    project start-up 131
    risks 44
    routine sales 17–18
    task list and work breakdown 68
Closedown see Project closure
Codes and coding systems
    benefits of a logical system 68, 75
    choosing a system 79
    cost codes 32, 80, 123,
        173, 175, 188
    customer's system compatibility
        80–81
    database application 75, 77
    functions of code 72
    need for simplicity 79–80
Coding examples
    heavy engineering project 76
    mining project 76
    radiocommunications project 73–5
Commissioning 12, 19, 21, 32, 59
Communicating and communications
    2, 6, 8, 19–20, 51, 55, 61,
    126, 134, 184, 200
Comparative cost estimates
    31–2, 34, 78–9
Computer planning and scheduling
    cost/time graph 117, 176
    filtering 119, 131–2
    Micro Planner X-Pert 88, 116

Microsoft Project 83, 116–17, 119
multi-project scheduling
    66, 135, 199
Open Plan (Deltek) 116,
    119, 135, 199
Primavera 107–8, 116–17,
    119–20, 199
Sorting 120
see also Calendars, Milestones,
    Work-to lists
Construction specification 22–3
Contingency allowance (contingency
    sum) 30, 39, 160, 191
Contract cost penalties 9
Contractor's specification see
    Project specification
Contractor's strategy 21–3, 27
Cost analysis see Earned value analysis
Cost budgets see Budgets
Cost codes see Codes and
    coding systems
Cost control see Cost management
Cost cut-off at project closure 192
Cost escalation 30, 39, 175, 188, 191
Cost estimating 29–41
    abilities of different people 35–6
    accuracy 30–31
    after-issue costs 40
    below-the-line costs 38–40
    collecting departmental
        estimates 34
    contingency allowances 39
    correction factors 35
    cost escalation 39
    documentation 32–3
    foreign currencies 40
    forgotten tasks 32
    materials and equipment 36–8
    provisional sums 40
    reviewing 40–41
    software tasks 32
    standard tables 31
    units 34
    validity time limit 38

Cost penalties 9
Cost performance index
    (CPI) 181–3, 189
Cost/time relationship 9, 117, 176
Critical path networks
    arrow and precedence diagrams
        compared 87–8
    arrow diagrams (ADM) 88–91
    furniture project 94–6
    level of detail 95, 97
    precedence diagrams
        (PDM) 91, 94–9
    role in resource scheduling 104
    time analysis 89–91, 93–4
    see also Float, Furniture project case
        study, Garage Project case study,
        Milestones, Resource scheduling
Customers' coding and numbering
    systems 79–81
Customer's specification *see*
    Project specification
Cybernetic control loop 134

Defining the project *see*
    Project definition
Definitive cost estimates 31
Design freeze 167, 184
Design specification 165
    see also Project specification
Design standards 127, 131
Direct costs
    control factors 198
    definition 29
    effect of delays on 8, 196
Document distribution 126–7

Earned value analysis 180–89
    actual cost of work performed
        (ACWP) 181–2, 188–9
    brick wall project case 182–3
    budget cost of work performed
        (BCWP) 181, 183, 188
    budget cost of work scheduled
        (BCWS) 181

cost performance index
    (CPI) 181–3, 189
    profitability prediction 142, 187–9
    schedule performance
        index (SPI) 181
Emergency modifications 167
    see also Kosy-Kwik
Engineering changes *see* Changes
Estimating *see* Cost estimating
Exceptions and exception reports 141–2
    see also Management by
        exception *and* Variances
Expediting purchases 143, 145,
    152–3, 155, 157

Failure mode and effect analysis
    (FMEA) 44–5
Failure mode effect and criticality
    analysis (FMECA) 45–6
Family tree *see* Work breakdown
    structure
Feasibility studies 5, 15, 17
Feedback in progress management
    51, 133–6
Fixed costs *see* Indirect costs
Fixed-price contracts 16–17, 22, 84
Float 90–91, 933
    free 110–11, 116, 168
    independent 111
    negative 112, 117, 138
    remaining 104, 111
    total 91, 110
    see also Critical path networks
Foreign currencies 40, 147, 175
Free float 110–11, 116, 138
Freight forwarding 98, 150, 154
Functional matrix organization
    52, 130
Furniture project case study
    as bar chart 84–6
    as critical path network 94–6

Gantt charts *see* Bar charts
Gantt, Henry 83

Garage project case example 104–14
Goes-into chart *see* Work
    breakdown structure
Goods inwards inspection
    141, 145, 155

Hybrid organization 59–60

Inconsistent estimators 36
Incoterms 150–51
Independent float 111
Indirect costs (overheads) 29, 38,
    175, 189, 195, 197–8
In-house projects 123, 196
    see also Management change
    and IT projects
Inspection and expediting 152–3
Insurance 19, 37, 43, 49, 50, 129,
    143, 147, 175, 189
Interchangeability rule 167
International Association of Project
    Management (IPMA) 12
International terms of trade
    (Incoterms) 150–51

Joint venture 48, 61–2

Kick-off meeting 24, 130, 141
Kosy-Kwik case study 168–71

Level of detail in network
    diagrams 95, 97, 132
Linked bar charts 85, 94

Management by exception
    134, 142, 155, 196–7
Management by surprise 134
Management by walking
    about 63, 136–7
Management change and IT
    projects 3, 11–12, 18, 199
    checklists for 20
Managing changes *see* Changes
    and modifications

Managing costs *see* Cost management
Managing progress *see* Progress
    management
Managing purchasing *see* Purchasing
    and materials management
Marked-up drawings 168, 170
Material and equipment costs
    34, 37, 117, 175
Materials shortages 8, 143, 155, 196
Matrix organization 54–5, 58, 60–61
Matrix versus team 57–9
Meetings *see* Kick-off meeting,
    Progress meetings
Micro Planner X-Pert 88, 116
Microsoft Project 83, 116–17, 119
Milestone analysis 176–80
Milestones 8, 11, 98–9, 119,
    131, 176, 190
Minutes of progress meetings 140
Modifications *see* Changes
    and modifications
Motivation 56–9, 130, 139, 184, 200

Negative float 112, 117, 138
Network analysis *see* Critical path
    networks, Float, Time analysis
Not invented here 21–2
Numbering systems *see* Coding
    and Coding examples

Objectives *see* Project objectives
Open Plan 116, 119, 135
Optimistic estimators 35
Organization
    balanced matrix 54, 58
    coordinated matrix (or
        coordination matrix) 52
    contract matrix 60–61
    hybrid 59–60, 65
    joint venture 2, 48, 61–2
    line and function 51–2
    secondment matrix 55
    task force 56
    team 55

team versus matrix 57–8
weak matrix 54
Overhead costs *see* Indirect costs
Overtime 99, 114–15

PDM (precedence diagram) *see*
    Critical path networks
Penalty clause 9, 169–70
Performance analysis *see* Earned
    value analysis
Pessimistic estimators 35
Physical project preparations and
    organization 128–9
Planning *see* Bar charts, Critical
    path networks, Computer
    planning and scheduling, Float,
    Furniture project case example
    and Resource scheduling
Post mortem 194
    Kozy-Kwik case 170
Precedence diagrams (PDM) *see*
    Critical path networks
Predicting profitability 187–9
Preliminary organization 124–8
Primavera 107, 199
Procurement *see* Purchasing and
    materials management
Product specification 21, 23, 26–7
Profitability prediction 187–9
Progress assessment 86, 188
Progress management 133–7
    as a closed loop control
        system 133–4
    corrective actions 133, 137–9
    feedback 51, 133–5, 156
    global checks 78, 137
    monitoring and schedule
        updating 134–7
    use of work-to lists 97, 116,
        120–21, 131–3, 135, 141
    when the news is bad 137–9
Progress meetings
    frequency of 139
    keeping meetings to the subject 139

minutes 140
Progress meetings abandoned 140–41
Progress reports
    exception reports 141–2
    external reports for clients
        and customers 142
    internal reports for company
        management 141
Project authorization 123–4
Project closure 192–4
    closure documentation 192–3
    cost cut-off 192
    post mortem 194
Project correspondence 126–7
Project definition 15, 30
Project handbook 127
Project ledger concept 186–7
Project life cycle (and life
        history) 4–5, 121
    impact of changes in
        relation to 159–60
Project Management
        Institute (PMI) 13
Project management office (PMO) 60,
        65, 132, 162, 164, 178, 197
Project manager
    as a hunter-gatherer of
        information 62–3
    current awareness 31, 63
    in the organization 51–5
    perceptiveness 3, 136
    support for 64, 195–201
    training 64–5
Project numbering 73, 123–4, 192
Project objectives 6, 123, 164, 184
    see also Triangle of objectives
Project organization *see* Organization
Project planning *see* Bar charts, Critical
    path networks, Computer
    planning and scheduling, Float,
    Furniture project case example
    and Resource scheduling
Project procedures manual
        (project handbook) 127

Project progressing *see* Progress
    management
Project registration 65, 123–4
Project room (war room) 55–6, 199
Project scheduling *see* Critical
    path networks, Bar charts
    and Resource scheduling
Project scope 15, 19–21, 23
Project services groups *see* Project
    Management Office (PMO)
Project specification 5, 7,
    21–7, 31, 130, 164
    see also Bikes 'n' Skates
        Project case example
Project success or failure
    factors 5–6, 9–11
Project task force 56
Project team organization
    55–9, 65, 184
Project types 2–3
Project variation orders (contract
    variation orders) 163–4,
    166, 174, 186, 197
    see also Changes
Project war room 55–6, 199
Projects difficult or impossible
    to define 3, 16–17
Provisional cost items and provisional
    sums 16–17, 30, 39–40
Purchase specifications 78, 98,
    145–6, 154, 156
Purchasing and materials
    management 143–56
    bid summary 147–50
    budgets 124
    contractual conditions 151
    early ordering of long-
        lead items 146–50
    expediting 152–3
    freight forwarding agents 154
    goods receipt 155
    Incoterms 150–51
    inspection and expediting
        visits 152

invitation to tender (ITT)
    98, 112, 146–50
obtaining bids 98
purchase enquiries 98, 112, 146–50
purchase order amendments
    25, 151–2, 164
purchase orders 37–8, 98–9, 145,
    150–51, 154–6, 163–4, 176, 192
purchase requisitions
    78, 145–6, 150
purchase specifications 78,
    98, 145, 154, 156
risk of duplicated orders 131
sealed bids 145, 147–8
shipping, port and customs
    formalities 153–4
shortages and shortage lists 155–6
supplier selection 145–50
vendors' documents 156–7
Purpose of project management 1

Quality/cost relationship 7

Remaining float 104, 111
Resource scheduling 30, 33, 65, 78,
    87, 101, 103–21, 131–3, 135
Responsibility matrix 124, 126
Risk and risk management 43–50
    appraisal and analysis 44–6
    failure mode and effect
        analysis (FMEA) 44–5
    failure mode effect and criticality
        analysis (FMECA) 45–6
    identification and listing 43–4
    insurance 49–50
    methods for dealing
        with risk 47–50
    qualitative assessment 44–5
    quantitative assessment 45–6
    register (risk log) 46–7
S curves 174
Schedule performance index
    (SPI) 181, 183–4
Scheduling cash flow *see* Cash flow

Scheduling resources *see*
　　Resource scheduling
Scientific research projects 2–3
Scope creep 73
Seven logical steps of scheduling 121
Shipping, port and customs
　　formalities 154
　freight forwarding 98, 150, 154
　Incoterms 150
　responsibility for 150
Slack *see* Float
Slack *see* Float
Stable design (design freeze) 167
Stage-gating (or stage-gate
　　control) 3, 16
Stage payment certification 61
Stakeholders 1, 9–12, 27, 195
Standard estimating tables 31

Target dates 112, 131, 133
Task force 56
Task list 32, 84, 105, 107
Team organization 55, 130, 184
Terms of trade (Incoterms) 150–51
Time/cost relationship 7–9
Time is money 7, 26

Time-limited resource
　　scheduling 113–15
Time-now date 86, 136
Total float 91–2, 94–5, 110–11, 138
Training
　customer staff 21,32
　project manager 56, 64–5
　project staff 48, 56
Triangle of objectives 6
Turnkey operation 21

Unfunded changes 160, 184

Variable costs *see* Direct costs
Variances (exceptions) 134, 141–2
Vendors' documents 156–7

War room *see* Project room
Work breakdown structure
　　(WBS) 67–81, 186
　　see also Codes and coding systems
　　and Coding examples
Work in progress 8, 25, 43, 166,
　　180–81, 189, 196, 200
Work-to lists 97, 116, 120–21,
　　131–3, 135, 140–41

If you have found this book useful you may be interested in other titles from Gower

Gower Handbook of People in Project Management
Edited by
Dennis Lock and Lindsay Scott
Hardback: 978-1-4094-3785-7
e-book: 978-1-4094-3786-4 (PDF)
e-book: 978-1-4724-0299-8 (ePUB)

Project Management
Dennis Lock
Hardback and CD-ROM: 978-1-4094-5419-9
Paperback: 978-1-4094-5269-0
e-book: 978-1-4094-5420-5 (PDF)
e-book: 978-1-4094-7476-0 (ePUB)

Naked Project Management:
The Bare Facts
Dennis Lock
Hardback: 978-1-4094-6105-0
e-book: 978-1-4094-6106-7 (PDF)
e-book: 978-1-4094-6107-4 (ePUB)

Visit **www.gowerpublishing.com** and

- search the entire catalogue of Gower books in print
- order titles online at 10% discount
- take advantage of special offers
- sign up for our monthly e-mail update service
- download free sample chapters from all recent titles
- download or order our catalogue